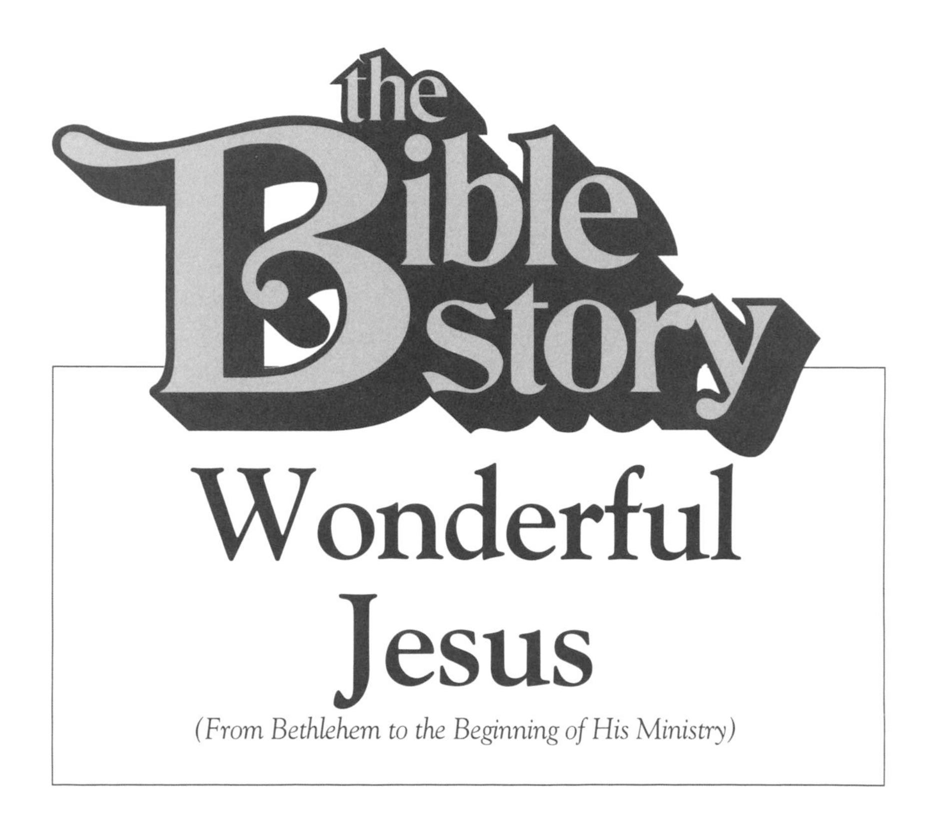

Wonderful Jesus

(From Bethlehem to the Beginning of His Ministry)

VOLUME SEVEN

the Bible Story

Wonderful Jesus ❖ Volume Seven

Arthur S. Maxwell
Author of Uncle Arthur's *Bedtime Stories*

When Arthur S. Maxwell wrote *The Bible Story,* he used the King James Version of the Bible, closely following its narrative. This edition continues that tradition and draws from other translations using language that today's children readily understand.

NEWLY REVISED AND ILLUSTRATED

More than 400 stories in 10 Volumes Covering the Entire Bible From Genesis to Revelation

REVIEW AND HERALD® PUBLISHING ASSOCIATION
HAGERSTOWN, MD 21740

Illustrations not individually credited are by Kreigh Collins, Russell Harlan, William Heaslip, William Hutchinson, Manning de V. Lee, Lester Quade, Paul Remmey, and Herbert Rudeen.

This book was
Revised by Cheryl Holloway
Edited by Eugene Lincoln
Cover art by Harry Anderson

PRINTED IN U.S.A.

R&H Cataloging Service
Maxwell, Arthur Stanley, 1896-1970
The Bible story.
1. Bible stories. I. Title.
II. Holloway, Cheryl Woolsey, 1956-
220.9505

ISBN 0-8280-0801-9

The impress of perfection was upon the character of Jesus even as a boy—a gracious disposition, a patience that nothing could disturb, and willing hands ever ready to serve others.

PAINTING BY HARRY ANDERSON

CONTENTS

PART ONE—Stories of Jesus as a Baby

Matthew 1:1-2:21; Luke 1:1-2:40

1. The Baby Everybody Wanted 9
2. Great News From Heaven 13
3. Two Happy Mothers 18
4. The Wonderful Name 23
5. Just in Time! 27
6. "No Vacancy" 31
7. Night of Nights 35
8. This Is the One! 43
9. Strangers From the East 47
10. Narrow Escape 53

PART TWO—Stories of Jesus' Boyhood

Luke 2:41-52

1. Journey to Egypt 59
2. Happy Days in Nazareth 63
3. First Big Holiday 69
4. Teaching the Teachers 74
5. Lost Boy Found 80
6. The Carpenter's Son 85

PART THREE—Stories of Jesus' Ministry

Matthew 3:1-4:22; Mark 1:1-20; Luke 3:1-4:13; John 1:1-4:42

1. Exciting News 93
2. The Shining Light 97
3. A Voice From Heaven 100
4. The Lamb of God 105
5. Battle in the Wilderness 109
6. Three Terrible Temptations 113
7. First Disciples 119
8. Jesus Begins to Preach 126
9. Wedding Surprise 129
10. The Temple Cleansed 134
11. Midnight Visitor 139
12. Sudden Harvest 145

PART FOUR—Stories of Jesus' Miracles

Matthew 4:23-25; 8:5-34; Mark 1:21-2:12; 4:35-5:20;
Luke 4:14-5:11;7:1-17; 8:22-40; John 4:43-54

1. Daddy's Prayer Answered 153
2. Madman in Church 157
3. Flood Tide of Love 160
4. Hometown Boy Returns 165
5. The Master Fisherman 169
6. The Man With Five Friends 174
7. The Centurion's Servant 177
8. The Interrupted Funeral 180
9. Lord of the Winds and Waves 184
10. Madmen Made Sane 189

PART ONE

Stories of Jesus as a Baby

(Matthew 1:1-1:21; Luke 1:1-2:40)

The Baby Everybody Wanted

DID YOU ever want a baby brother—or a baby sister—to come to your home? If so, you know how eagerly you looked forward to his coming, and how happy you were when he arrived. And you loved him because he was yours, your very own.

There was one baby Boy, however, whom everybody wanted. For hundreds of years fathers and mothers, brothers and sisters, hoped that this very special Baby would come to their home.

For a long time nobody knew just when or where He would be born, so Jewish parents everywhere kept wondering, Will He come to our home? And every little girl hoped that she would grow up to be the mother of this Baby.

You see, this Baby was part of a promise made by God in the Garden of Eden, when Adam and Eve had made their sad mistake. After God had told them that they must leave their beautiful home, He said to the snake who had caused all the trouble, "I will put enmity between you and the woman, and

← PAINTING BY HARRY ANDERSON

As Mary looked upon this lovely babe in her arms, and pondered the far-reaching prophecy of Simeon, she was full of grateful joy and hope that here at last was Israel's Deliverer.

Genesis 3:15

between your offspring and hers; he will crush your head, and you will strike his heel." [1]

This meant that someday a child, or grandchild, or great-grandchild of Eve's would "crush," the head of the wicked snake and undo all the evil he had done. Someday a wonderful Baby would be born who would break the power of Satan and regain all that people had lost because of sin.

Eve thought that she would be the mother of this Baby. When Cain was born she said, "With the help of the Lord I have brought forth a man." [2] But Cain was not the one. He turned out to be a murderer and killed his brother Abel.

After Abel's death Eve had another little boy and called him Seth, meaning "the appointed one." But again she was mistaken. He was not the Appointed One.

Of course Eve had baby girls too. And without doubt she told all of them about God's promise. So when each girl grew up and married, she hoped that she would be the mother of the wonderful Baby who would do all the glorious things God had spoken of. But all were mistaken.

They passed on the promise to their little girls, however, who told it to their little girls, who told it to their little girls, and so on down the years. In this way the hope of a coming Saviour and Deliverer was kept alive from century to century.

Moses knew about the promise. He said to the children of Israel: "The Lord your God will raise up for you a prophet like

Deuteronomy 18:15

Numbers 24:17

Isaiah 7:14

me from among your own brothers. You must listen to him." [3]

Balaam knew about it too, for instead of cursing Israel, as Balak wanted him to, he said, "A star will come out of Jacob; a scepter will rise out of Israel." [4] By this he meant that Someone was coming who would be both a light and a king; and people wondered even more when the promised Child would come.

The prophet Isaiah was more definite. He wrote: "The virgin will be with child and will give birth to a son, and will call him Immanuel." [5] Again, "To us a child is born, to us a son is given, and the government will be on his shoulders." [6]

After this, many who had lost hope hoped again. Many a young mother, looking down at her precious baby boy, must have asked, Could this be the One? Will my boy grow up to be the great Leader whom God has promised to send?

Micah 5:2

Then the prophet Micah revealed the very place where the Child was to be born. From home to home, and especially from mother to mother, the news spread like wildfire: "But you, Bethlehem Ephrathah, though you are small among the clans of Judah, out of you will come for me one who will be ruler over Israel." [7]

All eyes turned toward Bethlehem. For a little while every mother and child in or near the city became important. But nothing happened. And as the years rolled by, Micah's prophecy was forgotten. The few who remembered it thought he must have been mistaken.

Daniel 9:25

Then, after the Jews had been taken away into captivity and everybody was discouraged, another prophet brought thrilling news about the Baby. Daniel claimed that the angel Gabriel had revealed to him the exact time when the great Deliverer would appear.

Gabriel, he said, had told him that "from the issuing of the decree to restore and rebuild Jerusalem until the Anointed One, the ruler, comes, there will be seven 'sevens,' and sixty-two 'sevens.' "[8]

This was the most definite word yet. From the time that the king of Persia should order the rebuilding of Jerusalem to the coming of "the Anointed One, the ruler" would be 69 weeks (seven plus 62).

Sixty-nine weeks! That's no time at all, people said. He'll be here in less than two years! But others said the weeks must be "prophetic weeks," with each day reckoned as a year.

They were right. And this meant the world had to wait almost another 500 years. That is a long, long time, and as the years passed, Daniel's words were forgotten. People came to think that the wonderful Baby would never come.

Then, when many had given up hope altogether, something happened. The angel Gabriel came again, this time not to a prophet but to a girl. He brought great news from heaven.

---

[1] Genesis 3:15.
[2] Genesis 4:1.
[3] Deuteronomy 18:15.
[4] Numbers 24:17.
[5] Isaiah 7:14.
[6] Isaiah 9:6.
[7] Micah 5:2.
[8] Daniel 9:25.

Great News From Heaven

(Luke 1:26-38)

AS THE time drew near for the birth of Jesus there must have been great excitement among the angels in heaven. To them this was the most important event of the ages.

The Lord, whom they adored, was about to leave the realms of glory to go and dwell on one of the smallest planets He had created. To show how much He loved all His creatures, even those who had rebelled against Him, He was going to wrap Himself up in a little bundle of human flesh and live as a man among the people He had created.

How much the angels understood about this miracle of miracles we do not know, but it must have seemed to them the highest proof that God is love. They were so touched by this kind act that they wanted to tell everybody the wonderful news. How they must have wondered why the people on the earth—except for a very few—did not give a thought to His coming! Nobody was preparing a welcome for Him.

Eagerly they watched as the 483 years of Daniel's prophecy

gradually came to a close. Then, at exactly the right time—not a moment too soon, not a moment too late—God called upon Gabriel to fly swiftly to the earth and find a girl named Mary.

Just why God chose Mary the Bible does not say. But we do know that "the eyes of the Lord range throughout the earth to strengthen those whose hearts are fully committed to him." * No doubt Mary was the best girl He could find in all the world just then. He had been watching her all her life and knew that her heart was "fully committed to him." He believed He could trust her with this very great honor.

Of course He knew exactly where she lived—the very town, the very street, the very house, the very room. So when Gabriel drew near to Nazareth, he made no mistake. A moment later he was beside her.

"Greetings, you who are highly favored!" he said, so kindly and tenderly. "The Lord is with you."

Mary wondered who her visitor might be and what he meant by these strange words. How could she be "highly favored"—she, an unknown girl in an out-of-the-way village like Nazareth!

Seeing how frightened she was, Gabriel spoke more gently still. "Do not be afraid, Mary," he said, "you have found favor with God. You will be with child and give birth to a son, and you are to give him the name Jesus.

"He will be great and will be called the Son of the Most High. The Lord God will give him the throne of his father David, and he will reign over the house of Jacob forever; his kingdom will never end."

← PAINTING BY RUSSELL HARLAN

Gabriel made the astonishing announcement: "Fear not, Mary: for thou hast found favour with God. And, behold, thou shalt . . . bring forth a son, and shalt call his name Jesus."

This didn't seem possible to Mary. Her son to be a king! To sit on David's throne! To reign forever! Oh, no! She must be dreaming. Anyway, it couldn't happen, because she wasn't married. She was engaged to Joseph, that was all, and she told Gabriel so, in case he didn't know it.

Of course Gabriel knew it, and he was ready with his answer. If Mary was willing, he said, something very, very wonderful would happen to her. In perhaps the most beautiful words to be found in all the Bible, he said to her, "The Holy Spirit will come upon you, and the power of the Most High will overshadow you. So the holy one to be born will be called the Son of God."

Seeing that Mary still doubted, he told her a secret that must have surprised her very much. "Even Elizabeth your relative is going to have a child in her old age, and she who was said to be barren is in her sixth month."

"Elizabeth is having a baby!" I can hear Mary whispering to herself. "Not Elizabeth! And how does this stranger know that it's going to be a boy?"

Gabriel smiled. "Nothing is impossible with God," he said.

Mary bowed her head. " 'I am the Lord's servant,' " Mary answered. " 'May it be to me as you have said.' "

A moment later Gabriel vanished, and Mary was left alone wondering what it all meant and what was going to happen to her. Like many other God-fearing girls in Israel, she had thought how honored she would be if she could be the mother of the wonderful Baby so many people had been expecting for

hundreds and hundreds of years. But she had never dared to hope it might be so.

And now somebody—it must have been an angel—had told her that this Baby was going to be hers—hers! She was going to be the mother of the Messiah. Her son would be the great Deliverer of her people, the One the patriarchs and prophets had spoken about from the dawn of time. Yes! And He would be called "the Son of the Most High" and "the Son of God."

It was too wonderful to be real, too good to be true. Yet it was real and it was true. The wonderful Baby was on His way.

* 2 Chronicles 16:9.

Two Happy Mothers

(Luke 1:5-20, 39-79)

"ELIZABETH!"

"Mary!"

Surprise and happiness were in their eager greeting. Though close relatives, they had not seen each other for some time. Travel was difficult in those days. There were no cars, of course. One had to go from place to place on donkeyback or on foot, or not at all.

Mary had been so anxious to find out whether the mysterious stranger had told the truth about Elizabeth that she had hurried to the town in Judea where Elizabeth and her husband Zechariah (NIV) lived. When she saw Elizabeth, Mary realized at once that Gabriel had made no mistake.

What a story Elizabeth had to tell! She said that for a long time she and her husband had been praying that they might have a baby, but none had come. Then one day, about six months before, when Zechariah was busy with his priestly duties in the Temple, an angel had appeared to him. "Do not be afraid, Zechariah," the angel had said, "your prayer has been heard. Your wife Elizabeth will bear you a son, and you are to give him the name John."

"And you'll never guess what else he said about the baby," Elizabeth went on. "He told my husband that 'he will be great in the sight of the Lord. He is never to take wine or other fermented drink, and he will be filled with the Holy Spirit even from birth. Many of the people of Israel will he bring back to the Lord their God. And he will go on before the Lord, in the spirit and power of Elijah, to turn the hearts of the fathers to their children and the disobedient to the wisdom of the righteous —to make ready a people prepared for the Lord.'

"My husband," Elizabeth continued, "told the angel he didn't see how this could happen, because we are both getting on in years. But the angel replied, 'I am Gabriel. I stand in the presence of God, and I have been sent to . . . tell you this good news.'

"Then he said that my husband would be silent and not able to speak until the baby was born. And he's still unable to speak."

Then Mary told *her* story, sure now that it was Gabriel who had spoken to her.

Elizabeth listened with growing surprise. Suddenly she caught the full meaning of Gabriel's message. "Blessed are you among women, . . ." she said to Mary. "But why am I so favored, that the mother of my Lord should come to me?"

Then the Holy Spirit came upon Mary, and she spoke these beautiful words of praise to the One who had honored her so greatly. "My soul glorifies the Lord and my spirit rejoices in God my Savior, for he has been mindful of the humble state of his servant. From now on all generations will call me blessed, for the Mighty One has done great things for me—holy is his name.

"His mercy extends to those who fear him, from generation to generation. He has performed mighty deeds with his arm; he has scattered those who are proud in their inmost thoughts.

"He has brought down rulers from their thrones but has lifted up the humble.

"He has filled the hungry with good things but has sent the rich away empty.

"He has helped his servant Israel, remembering to be merciful to Abraham and his descendants forever, even as he said to our fathers."

Mary stayed in the home of Zechariah for three months, until it was time for Elizabeth's baby to be born.

There was quite a fuss then about naming the baby. Elizabeth said he was to be called John, but the neighbors insisted his name should be Zechariah, after his father. When they asked Zechariah, he still couldn't speak, but he made signs that he wanted to say something. They brought him writing material and this is what he wrote: "His name is John."

At once his voice returned, "and he began to speak, praising God." Then he told the neighbors all that had happened the day Gabriel spoke to him in the Temple. They were amazed and said to one another, "What then is this child going to be?"

Zechariah, now filled with the Holy Spirit, went on, "Praise be to the Lord, the God of Israel, because he has come and has redeemed his people. He has raised up a horn of salvation for us in the house of his servant David (as he said through his holy prophets of long ago), salvation from our enemies and from the hand of all who hate us—to show mercy to our fathers and to remember his holy covenant, the oath he swore to our father Abraham: to rescue us from the hand of our enemies, and to enable us to serve him without fear in holiness and righteousness before him all our days.

"And you, my child," he said, looking down lovingly at little John, "will be called a prophet of the Most High; for you will go on before the Lord to prepare the way for him, to give his people the knowledge of salvation through the forgiveness of their sins, because of the tender mercy of our God, by which the rising sun will come to us from heaven to shine on those living in darkness and in the shadow of death, to guide our feet into the path of peace."

I can almost feel the hush that came over the little group of people gathered round baby John as they listened to Zechariah. I think they sensed that a great moment in history had arrived.

It had. Heaven was drawing very near to earth. God had called for two baby boys. One was born, the other was on His way. One was to be "a prophet of the Most High," the other "the Son of the Most High." What a stir they would make when they grew up!

The Wonderful Name

(Matthew 1:21)

AFTER the birth of John, Mary returned to Nazareth where Joseph was waiting eagerly for her.

She had so much news to tell him! There was Gabriel's visit to Zechariah; Elizabeth's surprise at getting a baby; how John got his name; and finally Gabriel's strange and thrilling message to her.

As Joseph listened he became very worried. He didn't know what to make of it—especially the news about Mary having a baby. It was so unusual that he could hardly believe it. Was Mary telling him the truth? Had she really seen an angel? Would her baby be the Son of God and the king of Israel? How strange!

But God knew his thoughts, and that very night He sent Gabriel to speak to him in a dream. Gabriel told him that he did not need to worry. What had happened to Mary was according to God's plan. What's more, he said, "She will give birth to a son, and you are to give him the name Jesus, because he will save his people from their sins."

When Joseph awoke next morning, I am sure he told Mary all about his dream. I can almost hear him saying, "Gabriel has spoken to me too. He told me that your story is true, and he wants me to call the Baby 'Jesus.' "

"He told me the same thing," Mary may well have said.

"But there's nobody in our family by that name."

"I know. Surely it must have some special meaning."

"It does; it means 'Saviour.' This Child, Gabriel

said, is to 'save His people from their sins.' "

I am sure neither Joseph nor Mary understood fully what Gabriel meant. Not then. Like the rest of the people of Israel, they hoped someone would come to save them from the Romans—from the cruelty of their soldiers and the meanness of their tax collectors. But they never thought that such a person would save them from their *sins*. How would that help? But God knew that if Israel was saved from their sins, all their other troubles would come to an end.

In these wonderful words Gabriel tried to tell Joseph and Mary the most precious secret ever told. He wanted them to be the first to know that this Baby Boy who was coming to them was the very One who would break the power of Satan, as God had promised. This precious Child would grow up to be the Saviour of the world. He would help people to stop doing wrong. He would make them good and true and noble. And one day He would lead them back to long-lost Eden and restore everything that Satan took away.

"You are to give Him the name Jesus," said Gabriel, so that

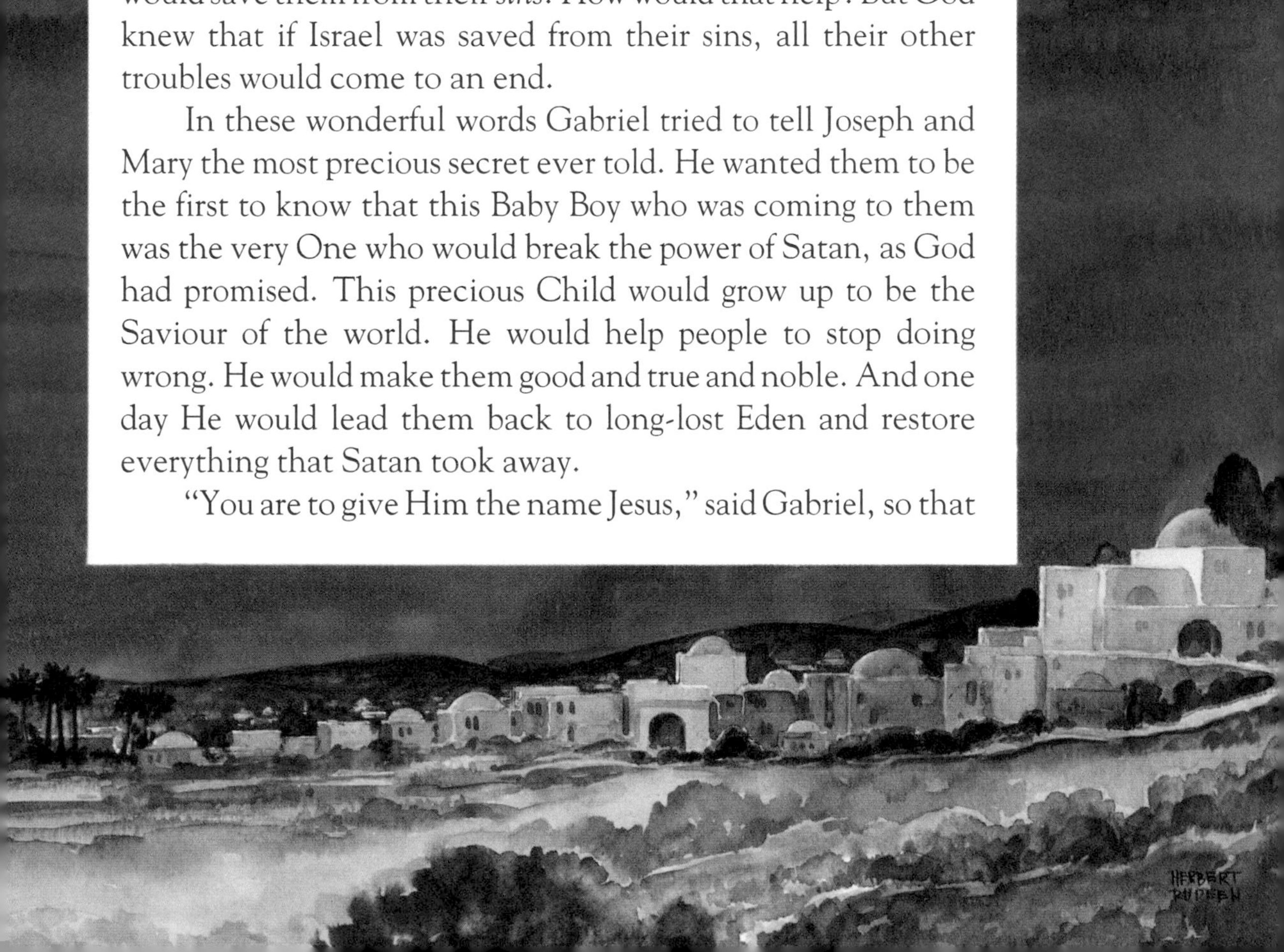

every time anyone called Him by this name, they would think of Him as a Saviour. His name would help them remember that He is able and willing to save them from the worst of sins.

"You are to give him the name Jesus," so that people of all nations would think of Him as One who would help them in every time of need.

"You are to give him the name Jesus," so that hope might come to the hopeless and joy to the sad, to the ends of the earth and the end of time.

No wonder the prophet Isaiah said that "he will be called Wonderful Counselor." It is wonderful—the most wonderful name anyone ever was given.

"You are to give him the name Jesus, because he will save his people from their sins."

Two thousand years have passed since Gabriel spoke these words to Joseph, but they mean as much and more today. They glow more brightly every passing day. Their glorious message is for you, for me, for everybody. He *can* save us and He *will* save us if we will let Him. And He will save us from *all* our sins.

Just in Time!

(Luke 2:1-5)

SLOWLY the weeks passed as Mary looked forward to the day when her wonderful Baby would be born. I am sure she prayed over and over again that God would make her the best mother that ever was. She wanted so much to be worthy of the great honor He had shown her.

Then one morning there was wild excitement in the sleepy little village of Nazareth. Roman soldiers came galloping into the marketplace. They said they had orders from the emperor in Rome.

Soon everybody was running toward them, eager to find out what was going on. Boys and girls pushed through the gathering crowd to get a better view of the splendid uniforms the soldiers were wearing.

"This is a decree from Caesar Augustus," cried an officer, unrolling a scroll, which he began to read. "Every citizen is to make his way at once to his hometown to be registered."

As the people listened their hearts sank. They guessed this was part of a new plan to get more taxes out of them. But there was nothing they could do about it. They had to obey.

Joseph was very upset. Because he was of "the house and line of David," his hometown was Bethlehem, 80 miles (130 kilometers) or so away. The last thing he wanted to do just now was to take Mary all that way. Her baby was due any time, and Joseph was afraid something might go wrong.

Today, of course, one can travel from Nazareth to Bethlehem by car in a couple of hours, but in those days it meant a long, tiring journey on donkeyback over steep mountain trails and rough, rutted roads. Three or four miles (five to six and a half kilometers) an hour was top speed, which meant a four-day trip at least, with no nice motels to stay in at night.

Joseph and Mary must have talked it over very seriously. Should they stay in Nazareth and risk trouble with the Romans, or should they try to get to Bethlehem in time, trusting God to watch over them on the way?

They decided to go to Bethlehem. Mary was lifted carefully

onto a donkey, and Joseph either walked beside her or rode another animal. It was rough going, and Joseph no doubt often asked, "Are you all right, Mary? Are you sure?"

He must have wished that the donkey would move faster, too. Never, it seemed, had it gone so slowly. And never had there been so much traffic. So many people were on their way to register as the Romans had told them to do.

But if Joseph was worried, his concern was nothing compared to that of the watching angels. Better than anyone on earth, they knew that the wonderful baby was to be born in Bethlehem, not in Nazareth, or Jerusalem, or somewhere in between. God had said so through the prophet Micah. And so, somehow, it must surely happen. But here was Mary on donkeyback, miles away from Bethlehem, and time was running out fast. Would she make it?

Oh, that donkey! Why wouldn't it go faster! How they must have wanted to get behind it and push!

Mile after weary mile the two tired people traveled. At night they rested as best they could, moving on the next morning at dawn.

Two days passed.

Three days.

"Are you all right, Mary?"

"I think so—I hope so. Is there much farther to go?"

"Not far. It won't be long now."

Evening was drawing on again as they slowly passed Jerusalem, where the traffic was worse than ever. They had only six miles to go now.

Another hour went by. Darkness was falling. Soon pinpoints of light could be seen in the distance.

"Bethlehem!" cried Joseph.

"Thank God!" murmured Mary. "Bethlehem!"

They had made it—just in time.

"No Vacancy"

(Luke 2:5-7)

HAVE you ever been traveling late at night and found a "No Vacancy" sign on every motel? If so, you know how very tired it made you feel. The thought that there was no place to rest, nowhere to go, seemed just too much to take, didn't it?

Imagine, then, how poor Joseph and Mary felt when they reached the only inn in town and found it full to overflowing. "There was no room for them in the inn."

It wasn't the innkeeper's fault. He couldn't help it. Probably he was beside himself trying to find food, let alone rooms, for all the people crowding into the city to obey the decree of Caesar Augustus.

When he saw Mary and guessed what was the matter, I am sure he was sorry for her. Who would not have been? But what could he do? When a hotel is full, it's full, that's all.

Of course, if the innkeeper had known all Mary knew—that it was the Messiah Himself who was to be born that night—he would have found a place for her somewhere, even if he had to give up his own room. And here he missed a great blessing. What a story he would have had to tell for the rest of his life! How famous his inn would have become! People would have talked of his good fortune to the end of time.

By failing to do the best he could for a poor, needy girl, he lost a great opportunity. Jesus may well say to him someday, "Whatever you did not do for one of the least of these, you did not do for me." [1] How careful we should be when someone in need comes to us!

But in the hurry and bustle of the moment the innkeeper did not think of all this. Instead, he offered his stable.

"The stable!" said Joseph. "Is that all you have?"

"At least it's shelter, and better than nothing."

The stable! As Mary heard the word her heart sank. All day she had longed for a comfortable place to rest. Now there was nothing but a stable! Maybe she cried. I am sure she thought of what Gabriel had said to her: "He will be great and will be called the Son of the Most High. The Lord God will give him the throne of his father David, and he will reign over the house of Jacob forever; his kingdom will never end."

Could she have been mistaken? she wondered. If what Gabriel had said was true, why was there nothing ready for her Baby? Surely "the Son of the Most High" should not be born in a smelly old stable!

A door creaked in the darkness. Joseph went ahead with a lantern. A cow mooed. A horse neighed. A rooster crowed.

"This way," said Joseph. "There's some clean straw over here." Peering through the gloom, Mary saw an empty manger, half filled with hay for the cows to eat.

"This will do for the Baby," she said.

A manger! Yes, it would do. But what a strange place for "the Son of the Most High" to lie. He could not have chosen a humbler place for His coming into the world. Perhaps it was because He wanted the humblest and the poorest to know that He loved them and that He was willing to share their lot.

No red carpet was spread for Him when He came from heaven to earth. There was only the straw on a muddy floor.

No fine linen, no downy quilt, was provided for His bed—only the fragrant hay.

No trumpets blared a welcome when He came. There was no sound at all except the mooing of cows, the neighing of horses, the braying of donkeys, the barking of dogs, as the creatures of His creation tried their best to say, "We're glad you've come to see us."

Then it happened. The wonderful Baby was born. And they called Him Jesus.

Nobody was there except Joseph and Mary and the angels. Yet it was the most wonderful event in history. All heaven had waited thousands of years for this moment. Patriarchs and prophets had longed for it since the dawn of time. Yet nobody else was there. Few knew. Few cared.

In His infinite love the Son of God had stepped from heaven to earth to take on "human likeness" and "the very nature of a servant" [2] that He might be our Saviour and Redeemer; and here He was, lying in a manger. Here was the all-powerful Lord of Creation as weak and helpless as a little child. Here was the all-wise King Eternal, unable to speak a single word. Here was the Source of all life, dependent for food on a girl.

This was indeed "love divine, all loves excelling, joy of heaven, to earth come down." [3]

Don't you wish you could have been there to welcome Him? Just to say, "Thank You, dear Lord," for such love as this?

[1] Matthew 25:45.
[2] Philippians 2:7.
[3] Charles Wesley, "Love Divine."

Night of Nights

(Luke 2:8-20)

SUPPOSE you had been living in Bethlehem that night when Jesus was born. What would you have seen and heard?

Imagine for a moment you are there with your brother. It is a warm night, so you are lying on a bed on the roof of a flat-topped house. The rest of the family is asleep, but you are awake, looking up at the sky, trying to count the stars.

"I never saw so many people in our town," you say.

"I wonder how long they will stay?" says your brother.

"Till the taxing is over, I suppose."

There is silence for a moment.

"I've been wondering," you say.

"Wondering what?"

"About what Father has been telling us lately. You know, about the Messiah's coming. He says the time is nearly up, and the old prophecies must be fulfilled soon."

"Isn't He to come to Bethlehem?"

"Yes. He's to be born here. The prophet Micah says so. I wonder when?"

There is a pause. Then a cry. "Look at that! Up there in the sky!"

"What? Where?"

"The light! The beautiful light. What can it be?"

"Looks like a star. It's right over the inn. No, it isn't. It's over the stable behind the inn. What can be happening? Let's go and see! Quietly now. Don't wake everybody!"

Silently you both creep downstairs, cross the road, and walk toward the inn. Suddenly you stop, for the light seems to have moved outside the town.

You run past the guards at the gates and across the fields to the place where the shepherds keep their sheep at night. You see a group of men standing open-mouthed as a glorious being talks to them.

Can this be the Messiah? you wonder. Surely not. Then it

HERBERT
RUDEEN

must be an angel! You hear him saying, "Do not be afraid. I bring you good news of great joy that will be for all the people. Today in the town of David a Savior has been born to you; he is Christ the Lord."

"Did you hear that?" you ask. "He says Messiah is here—that He has just been born!"

"Sh-sh! Listen. The angel is speaking again."

"This will be a sign to you: You will find a baby wrapped in cloths and lying in a manger."

Suddenly you see a perfectly marvelous sight. Right before your eyes appears a multitude of shining angels, thousands upon thousands of them, all singing together, "Glory to God in the highest, and on earth peace to men on whom his favor rests."

The heavens are flooded with light. Everywhere it is as bright as day. You can see the rugged mountains all around, the awe-struck shepherds, the trembling sheep, and every building in Bethlehem. Oh, yes, and the angels. So many angels, all singing their loudest as though they had been waiting ages and ages to sing this song.

"Glory to God! Glory to God! Glory to God in the highest!" The majestic music seems to roll clear round the world and out toward the stars, "Glory to God in the highest!"

Then, more gently, "On earth peace to men." How tenderly and hopefully they sing these closing words of their lovely hymn of praise! It is as if they long to see people everywhere welcome their Saviour with open arms and make Him the Lord of their lives.

As suddenly as they came the angels disappear. Darkness settles again over the fields and hills. You watch the shepherds to see what they will do. You hear them say, "Let's go to Bethlehem and see this thing that has happened, which the Lord has told us about."

"Let's go at once!" they all cry, and you see them hurrying off toward the city gate, stumbling over rocks and briers in their haste. But they get up and hurry on, eager to tell the great news they have heard.

You run behind them to see where they will go.

They pass a sleepy-eyed citizen near the inn. "Was a baby born around here tonight?" a shepherd asks.

"Yes, down there in the stable."

They run on. It is still dark, though dawn is on the way. A dim light comes through cracks in the door.

And what is that? A baby's cry! This must be the place. They push open the door and peer in. You are right behind them.

HERBERT RUDEEN

At the far end a man is standing. Beside him is a young woman resting on a pile of straw. Beside her, in a manger, is a baby, wrapped in cloths.

Surely this must be the Baby the angel spoke about. And if so, He must be the promised Saviour, Christ the Lord!

Reverently the shepherds enter the stable. Joseph and Mary look up startled, wondering what these strange, rough men are doing here at this time of night. Have they come to turn them out?

No indeed! They have come to see the Baby.

One of the shepherds begins to explain. They were in the field, he says, keeping watch over their flocks at night, when all of a sudden they saw an angel, who told them that the Messiah had been born this very night, and they would find Him lying in a manger.

Mary's eyes glow. She understands. And she is glad. Now she is sure God has not forgotten her. He knows where the Baby is, even though He is lying in a manger.

Over and over again the shepherds tell their story, with first one, then another, breaking in to add some fresh detail about what happened that night. And all the while they keep looking down at the Baby and saying how lovely He is.

As it dawns on them more and more clearly that this really is the long-promised Messiah, the Son of the living God, they kneel beside the manger and worship Him, the first in all the world to do so.

Eventually they say goodbye to Joseph and Mary and go on their way. As they do, the sun is coming up over the mountains. A new day is dawning for Bethlehem and the world.

People are just waking up and getting breakfast. Some are taking care of their animals. They look at the shepherds in astonishment. Their faces glowing, these roughly dressed men are "glorifying and praising God" right in the main street! Eagerly they are stopping passersby and telling them about the marvelous things they saw and heard that night.

"You mean you saw angels?" somebody says to them.

"Angels here in Bethlehem?"

"Yes, indeed, 'a great company of the heavenly host . . . praising God and saying—' "

"Impossible!"

"But we did. They told us Messiah was born."

"Messiah born here last night! Oh, no. That couldn't be."

"It's true! He's in the stable over there behind the inn."

"And all who heard it were amazed at what the shepherds said to them." Some believed their story, others did not. Some went to the stable to see the Christ Child. Others didn't bother. They let the greatest event of the ages go right past them without a thought.

They busied themselves with their daily chores—washing dishes, cleaning house, feeding animals, making money—while the very One they said they wanted so much was so close by. How careful we should be not to let ourselves get so busy that we do not realize when Jesus is near!

Of those who went to the stable that morning, some saw just another baby, and some saw God. It has been that way ever since. It is that way still. As you look at Him today, whom do *you* see?

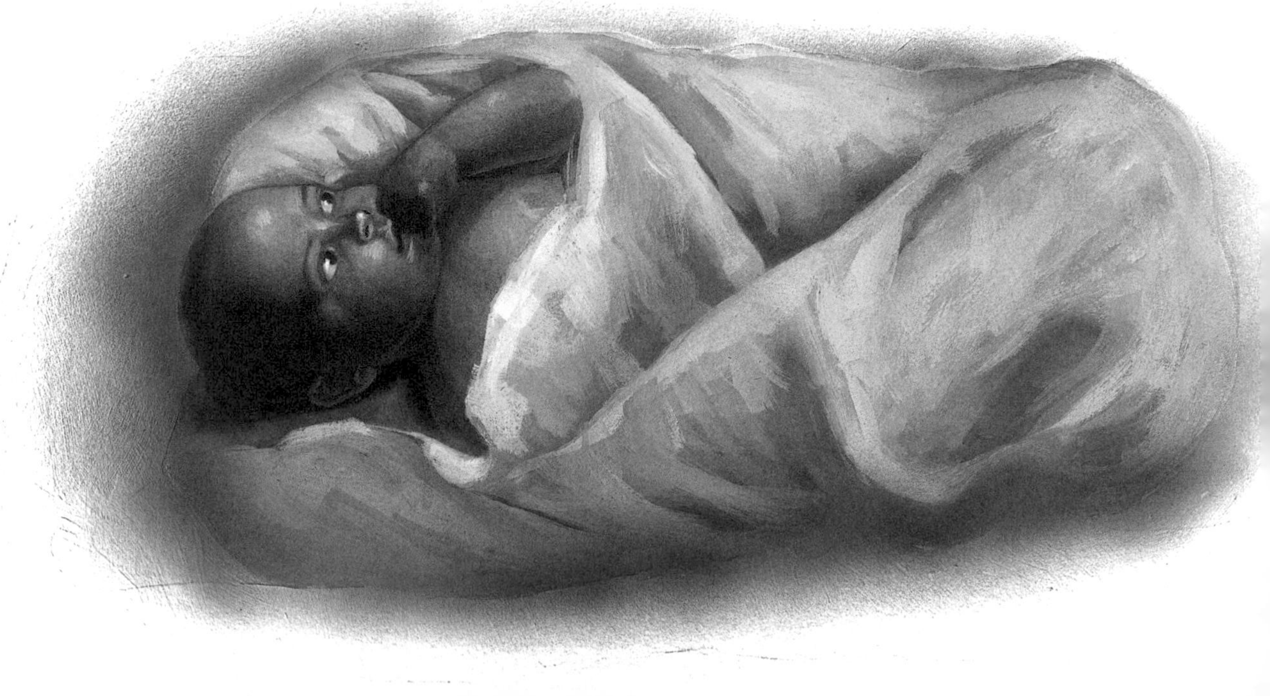

This Is the One!

(Luke 2:22-38)

IF YOU could have been in the Temple at Jerusalem about six weeks after Jesus was born, you would have seen a very old man. He was looking eagerly at the babies that mothers and fathers were bringing to the priests for dedication.

His name was Simeon, and he had been interested in babies for a long time now. Mothers loved the way he looked at their children, as though he really cared about them. They thought he must be a very kindhearted old man, and he was.

But he was more than just a kindly, grandfatherly person. He was a scholar, and he knew the Holy Scriptures from Genesis to Malachi. For years and years he had been looking for "the consolation of Israel." He had studied all the prophecies about the Messiah and was sure in his heart that the time had come for Him to appear. What's more, the Lord had told him that he would not die until he had seen the Child of promise.

That's why he looked so keenly at every baby brought to the Temple. Of course, the parents didn't know what was going on in his mind, but he was asking himself all the time, Could this be the one? Or this? Or this?

Many mothers and fathers came with their firstborn sons to dedicate them to God and offer thank offerings, and Simeon never tired of talking with them and looking at their babies. Day after day he searched for the One he longed to see.

One day as he entered the Temple, he noticed two people who had come to dedicate their little Son. He knew they were Galileans from their clothing. He could tell they were poor, because they were carrying two birds in a cage as their offering. "A pair of doves or two young pigeons" was the gift that only the poorest people were supposed to bring.

Simeon had never seen these people before, but there was something about them that interested him very much, particularly the young woman with the sweet, gentle face. Here, he felt sure, was one who loved the Lord. There was no doubt about that.

He looked down at the child, and suddenly his heart stirred. Somehow it came to him, all of a sudden. It was as though the voice of God had spoken to him saying, "This is the Messiah! This is the One for whom you have been looking so long!"

Tears of happiness rolled down the old man's cheeks. Taking the precious baby and holding Him close, he said, "Sovereign Lord, as you have promised, you now dismiss your servant in peace. For my eyes have seen your salvation, which you have prepared in the sight of all people, a light for revelation to the Gentiles and for glory to your people Israel."

Joseph and Mary looked on, amazed. The Bible says they marveled at the things Simeon was saying about their child. And Mary may well have said to herself, "How does he know? Did Gabriel tell him too?"

Then the old man turned to Joseph and Mary and blessed them. Looking into Mary's eager, upturned face, he spoke directly to her, saying, "This child is destined to cause the falling and rising of many in Israel, and to be a sign that will be spoken against, so that the thoughts of many hearts will be revealed. And a sword will pierce your own soul too."

Mary wondered what he meant. What strange destiny was ahead of her precious little Jesus? How would He cause people to fall and rise again? And what was this about a sword piercing her soul? Was not her child to become King of Israel? How could there be any suffering? Some day she would understand, but not now.

Hardly had she time to think about Simeon's strange words before an elderly woman came hurrying over to them. Her name was Anna. She was 84 years old and a prophetess. All excited, she took one look at Mary and her Baby, and began to thank God aloud that He had sent the Messiah at last. People around heard her and came to see what was going on. Eagerly Anna told her story and "spoke about the child to all who were looking forward to the redemption of Jerusalem."

Some believed her; others doubted; but most just said, "What a lovely baby!" and went on their way without giving the matter another thought.

But the words of Simeon and Anna meant a great deal to Mary. Now she was more sure than ever that her Baby was indeed the Messiah, the Child of promise and prophecy.

Strangers From the East

(Matthew 2:1-12)

HOW MANY people saw the wonderful light in the sky when the angels came to Bethlehem to rejoice over the birth of Jesus nobody will ever know. But we do know it was seen hundreds of miles away.

Far to the east of Palestine, possibly in Arabia or Persia, a little group of men not only saw the light but were convinced it had some special meaning. They were well-educated and wise and knew the Hebrew Scriptures well, for they were sure that the time had come for the king of Israel to appear.

They must have studied the prophecies of Daniel, Moses, Isaiah, and others. They had worked out the 70-week prophecy better than the leaders of Israel had done. And when they had read the promise "A star will come out of Jacob," they had looked not only for a king, but for a star.

When they saw the strange light they said to themselves, "This must be what we have been expecting." Then they set out to find what it meant. Day after day they journeyed until they came at last to Jerusalem.

To their surprise, they found all the people there going about their business as usual. Nobody was talking about the coming of a new king.

"Where is the one who has been born king of the Jews?" they asked someone.

"King of the Jews?" replied the man with a puzzled look on his face. "You mean Herod?"

"No. A new King. Your King. 'We saw his star in the east and have come to worship him.' "

"There's no new king around here," said the man.

"But there must be," said the Wise Men as they went on to tell why they had come so far. After a while a few people in Jerusalem began to believe that they must be right. Pretty soon the entire city was talking about these strangers who had traveled hundreds of miles to find the new King of the Jews.

When news of the Wise Men's story reached Herod, it sounded like treason. He was worried. Perhaps the Jews were about to rebel again, and this tall tale about a new king was part of the plot. So he called the "chief priests and teachers of the law" and demanded that they tell him "where the Christ was to be born."

"In Bethlehem in Judea," they told him, "for this is what the prophet has written: 'But you, Bethlehem, in the land of Judah, are by no means least among the rulers of Judah; for out of you will come a ruler who will be the shepherd of my people Israel.' "

Somehow, from the way the priests and teachers of the law

HERBERT RUDEEN

talked, Herod felt sure that *they* did not believe that any new King had been born. As far as they were concerned, their "ruler" might not appear in Bethlehem for hundreds of years yet. But Herod was troubled by the rumor that the Wise Men from the East had started. Was there anything to it? He would find out.

Herod sent for the Wise Men. They were still in town and came gladly. He treated them graciously and asked them to tell him exactly what they had told so many others. They did, and Herod listened with great interest. Then he asked, "When did you first see this star?"

They told him.

"And how long have you been on your way?"

They told him that too.

"Do you think that this new King is to be born in Bethlehem?"

"Certainly."

"And you believe He is already born?"

"The prophecies suggest it."

"H'm. I'll tell you what," said Herod. "You go to Bethlehem and find this Child. Then send me word, and I will come and worship Him also."

The Wise Men thanked the king and left. The great King Herod believed them! He wanted to worship the Baby too! With lighter hearts they set out for Bethlehem.

Then they saw something that made them overjoyed. There, in the sky above the little town, they saw the star again, the very one they had seen in the East many weeks ago. I can almost hear them saying to one another, "Look! There it is again!"

Now they urged their camels forward with new eagerness, sure that their search was almost at an end. As they clattered

HERBERT
RUDEEN

through the gates of David's city, people looked up and wondered who these wealthy-looking strangers might be. But the taxing had brought so many people, both rich and poor, to town that they took no special notice of them.

At last the Wise Men came to the house where Joseph and Mary were now staying. As they entered, "they saw the child with his mother Mary, and they bowed down and worshiped him."

What a sight that must have been as these Wise Men, dressed in their rich clothing, bent low before the Baby Jesus!

Imagine what Mary must have thought! Can't you see her eyes growing wide with amazement as the strangers opened up bags and boxes of various kinds and brought out treasures such as she had never seen before? Gold, incense, and myrrh were gifts fit for a king, and here they were being poured out before her little Boy! I think she must have cried in joy and gratitude.

"Thank you! Thank you!" I can hear her saying. "How kind of you to come so far and give us so much!"

Then they left and vanished into history. Nobody knows what happened to them. But the respect and love they showed their King will be remembered forever.

---

* Numbers 24:17.

Narrow Escape

(Matthew 2:12-18)

KING HEROD waited and waited for the Wise Men to return. But they never came.

They had planned to go home through Jerusalem, for they thought the king really wanted to find the Child and worship Him, as he had said. But the very night after they had visited Joseph and Mary, God warned them in a dream not to return to Herod. So "they returned to their country by another route."

For a while Herod was not worried. He had not believed the Wise Men's story about seeing a strange star in the sky, and he chuckled as he recalled sending them to Bethlehem to find a Baby who was to be King of the Jews. *Such a wild-goose chase!* he had thought. There couldn't be any such Child.

But after several days had passed and no word had reached him from the strangers, he decided to find out what they were doing. He sent messengers to Bethlehem to check on them. Then he learned that they had secretly left the city and gone home without saying a word to anybody.

Now Herod was angry. How could they have dared to go off like this! Why hadn't they told him the result of their search, as he had expected? He began to be suspicious. Perhaps they *had* found the Child they were looking for and wanted to keep the secret to themselves. Yes! That was it! They must be parties to a plot to set up a new king of Israel!

"All right!" the cruel king said to himself. "I'll fix that. No new king will come out of Bethlehem if I have anything to do with it."

In his rage he ordered a company of soldiers to go to Bethlehem and kill every child of 2 years old and younger. They were to do a thorough job. Not a single baby was to be spared.

It was a terribly wicked thing to do, and even the hardened soldiers must have hated doing it. Yet what could they do but obey? Sick at heart, but with swords sharpened, they set out for the doomed city.

But even as they clattered out of the gate of Jerusalem, all heaven moved into action to save the Baby Jesus. Herod had reckoned without God's secret service. Scarcely had his order been heard by the watching angels than one was quickly sent to the house where Joseph and Mary were staying.

It was night, and they were both asleep.

"Get up!" the angel said to Joseph. "Quickly! Take the young Child, and flee into Egypt. Stay there till I tell you. Herod is planning to destroy the Child."

Joseph awoke, sensing danger near. "Mary!" he cried. "Wake up!"

Mary stirred in her sleep. "What's the matter?" she asked.

"We must leave at once!"

"Why?"

"Herod wants to kill the Baby. An angel just told me."

"But why?"

"I don't know."

Mary rose to her feet, anxiety showing on her face. "But where can we go?"

"To Egypt. He said we would be safe there."

Quickly they dressed and packed their things, carefully

hiding the treasures the Wise Men had given them. Soon their donkey was loaded and they were on their way.

It was a narrow escape. They had not gone far when Herod's soldiers arrived and began breaking into people's homes. Heartlessly they tore the children from their mother's arms and killed them.

That was when Jeremiah's prophecy came true: "A voice is heard in Ramah, weeping and great mourning, Rachel weeping for her children and refusing to be comforted, because they are no more."

What a dreadful night that was! So many children murdered, so many homes left heartbroken!

Perhaps Baby Jesus—now on His way to safety—heard the cries of the mothers and babies of Bethlehem. He could not help them now, but some day He would be the comforter of Israel, the deliverer of all who would trust in Him.

PART TWO

Stories of Jesus' Boyhood

(Luke 2:41-52)

HERBERT
RUDEEN

Journey to Egypt

(Matthew 2:15, 19, 20)

SLOWLY, very slowly, Joseph and Mary made their way southward with their precious Baby. It was a long, tiresome journey, for much of the road passed through a dry, sandy desert, where there were no comfortable places for anybody to rest. It isn't much more than 100 miles (160 kilometers) from Bethlehem to the border of Egypt, and today you could travel that distance in a couple of hours; but in those days it meant several days' hard traveling.

Poor Mary! How she must have wondered why all this had to happen to her. Why did Herod want to kill her Baby? And if little Jesus was indeed the Son of the Most High, as Gabriel had told her, why couldn't she have a home in which to care for Him? Why did she have to wander about like this, owning nothing in the world but the few things tied on the donkey's back?

At last they crossed the border into Egypt. There was not much difference in the scenery—just more sand, more desert—

← PAINTING BY HERBERT RUDEEN

Joseph received warning to flee into Egypt with Mary and Jesus to escape the cruelty of Herod. Their way paid by the Magi's gifts, they set out by night to live among strangers.

but oh, what a relief to know that they were safe from Herod's soldiers at last!

How far they went into Egypt the Bible does not say, but they may well have passed the pyramids, which Abraham had seen when he came this way. And they must have walked by the Nile, where Moses was laid in the bulrushes when he was a baby.

Just where they lived in Egypt or how long they stayed there, nobody knows. It could be that Joseph got work as a carpenter to help pay expenses while Mary stayed in some humble home and cared tenderly for her Baby.

One night when Jesus was still a little boy, the angel of the Lord came again to Joseph, this time with good news. King Herod was dead, he said, and it was now safe for them to return to Palestine. "Get up," said the angel, "take the child and his mother and go to the land of Israel, for those who were trying to take the child's life are dead."

When Joseph told Mary what the angel had said, I can imagine she was delighted at the thought of going home. True, God had been good to them in Egypt. With the money Joseph had been able to earn and the gold that the Wise Men had given them, they had been able to live comfortably, although they had always felt they were strangers in a strange land. Never a day had passed but they had felt the tug of their homeland.

Now they could go back and see their friends and loved ones again. It was too good to be true!

Packing up once more, they prepared to leave the land that had sheltered them when they needed a refuge. One bright morning they set out northward, following—at least part of the way—much of the route that the Israelites traveled when Moses led them out of Egypt to Canaan.

Did you ever wonder what Jesus thought about it all? He had come into Egypt in His mother's arms, but He left it on His own sturdy little legs. Of course, He was too little to walk very far, and no doubt Joseph had to lift Him up on the donkey beside Mary every now and then to give Him a rest. But like every other healthy little boy, He was eager to act grown-up as much as possible.

He was just beginning to talk too, and probably asked an endless stream of questions. I can almost hear Him saying,

"What's that animal, Mamma? That one with the big hump on his back?"

"That's a camel, dear."

"And that one with the pointy things on its head?"

"That's an ox; and the pointy things are its horns."

"And what's that funny house over there?"

"That isn't a house, dear. It's a place where the Egyptians buried one of their kings, long, long ago. They call it a pyramid."

"Daddy, who's that lady lying down in front of the pyramid? She seems to be smiling at me."

"Oh, that's a very old statue cut out of rock. It's called the Sphinx."

So He chattered on, asking questions and questions and still more questions about everything He saw. Patiently Joseph and Mary answered them all as best they could.

Every now and then they tried to tell Him little bits of history that they thought He would understand—about how God had watched over His people in this very place and how He had brought them out of slavery into freedom in the happy, happy land where they were going now.

Happy Days in Nazareth

(Matthew 2:21-23; Luke 2:40)

MILE after mile Joseph and Mary journeyed back along the road they had traveled when they were running away from Herod. Somehow it didn't seem so far now, for they were going home, home, home!

At each stopping place Joseph asked other travelers for news, for there were no newspapers in those days. He had been away so long that he wanted to catch up on everything. What was the price of grain in Jerusalem? How much were carpenters earning nowadays? What had the Romans been doing lately?

One piece of news troubled him. Herod had been succeeded by his son Archelaus, who was reported to be as cruel as his father. Perhaps he too, was looking for the baby who had escaped from Bethlehem.

Joseph and Mary had planned to go and live in the little town where their precious Jesus had been born, but now this was impossible. So they decided to go on to Nazareth, which they had left at the time of the taxing by Caesar Augustus.

Some days later they arrived at their old hometown. All their old neighbors were glad to see them again. Joseph opened up his carpenter's shop, and Mary began housekeeping. As for Jesus, the Bible says that He "grew and became strong; he was filled with wisdom, and the grace of God was upon him."

What a fine boy He must have been! So strong, so healthy, so good-looking! With His perfect little body I am sure He could run faster and jump higher than any other boy or girl in town. With His marvelous eyesight and hearing He saw and heard everything that went on around Him. He missed nothing and stored up all sorts of priceless memories for use in days to come.

He grew not only in size like the other children of Nazareth, but in knowledge and wisdom too. His mother helped Him, of course. I am sure Mary took Him on many walks into the hills and fields around Nazareth, pointing out all the beauties of nature and answering His many, many questions about them.

What a privilege Mary had, showing the flowers, the trees, and the animals to Him who, long, long ago had created them! Perhaps this was why Jesus was so very interested in everything. Maybe deep down inside Him there was a strange feeling that somehow all these lovely things were really His and belonged to Him more than to anyone else in all the world.

Tenderly He would pick the lilies of the field and marvel at the beauty of their colors and the daintiness of their petals. Can't you hear Him saying to His mother, "Who made these beautiful things, Mamma?"

Watching a sparrow flit from tree to tree or counting the speckled eggs in a thrush's nest, He would tell Mary of the wonder that filled His heart. "How do little birds come from eggs, Mamma?" He would ask. "And how do they know how to fly?"

I wish I could have been there to hear Mary's answers, don't you? But I am sure she always talked to Him with great patience, always leading Him to honor and reverence His heavenly Father.

What wonderful bedtime stories Mary must have told Him before He went to sleep each night! I am sure she did her best to tell Him all she had ever heard or read about God's plan of salvation for the lost world. Beginning with the story of the Garden of Eden and how Adam and Eve lost their lovely home because of Satan's trickery and their own sad mistake, she went on to tell how God planned to make everything right again.

"They didn't lose it forever, darling," I can hear her saying. "Oh, no. For God promised to send a little boy someday who would grow up to be big and strong and good and take the lost world away from Satan and give it back to those who love and obey God."

And maybe Jesus said, with a faraway look, "I'd like to be that little boy, Mamma. I really would."

Then Mary would tell about Noah and the ark, the Flood and the rainbow—all those dear, sweet stories that mothers have told their children for thousands of years. And of course she told about Abraham, Isaac, and Jacob, and about Joseph and his brothers.

Then, too, there were the stories about Moses and how he led Israel out of Egypt through the Red Sea to Sinai, where God gave His people the Ten Commandments; about Joshua and the conquest of Canaan; about David and Solomon; about Daniel and Nehemiah.

Eagerly Jesus drank in every word. And when Mary would stop to say, "Now it's really time you went to sleep, dear," He would say, like any other little child of His age, "Oh, just one more, please, Mamma! Just one more!"

I suppose there were some stories He liked better than others, such as the one about the three Hebrews in the blazing furnace, or how Abraham started to offer up Isaac on the mountain when he saw a ram caught in a thicket.

Now and then that strange look would come back on His eager face again, as He would say, "Sometimes, Mamma, I almost think I was there. I can see it all so clearly."

Day after day Mary would read the Holy Scriptures to Him, especially the chapters in the Old Testament where the prophets wrote about the coming of the Messiah. Jesus heard them so often that He soon knew them by heart and where to find them.

Every Friday evening the little family would kneel in prayer together to welcome the holy Sabbath. The next morning they would go to the synagogue for worship. It was a custom with them. They never missed. The preacher was always sure that Joseph, Mary, and that wonderful little Boy of theirs would be in their places in the house of God.

How pleased the minister must have been to have a Boy like that in front of him—so interested, so atten-

tive, looking up with keen, wide-open eyes!

This was how Jesus became "strong" and "filled with wisdom." Knowledge of God's Word made Him strong and wise, and as a result "the grace of God was upon him."

He was gracious at home and at play with other children. He was kind and unselfish, always trying His best to be helpful. I am sure that Mary never had to ask Him twice to wash the dishes and that there was never a word of grumbling when Joseph sent Him on an errand.

No doubt He was teased by other children because He took a stand for right and truth, but nothing they said or did could make Him say or do anything wrong. Others might cheat or lie, or tell shady stories, but not Jesus. And they always knew He would never go back on His word.

Don't you wish you could have known Him then? I do. And wouldn't it be wonderful if you could be as good and kind and truthful and courteous as He was? You can be if you want to be. This same Jesus, now Lord of glory, will help you if you ask Him. He understands all your problems, because, you see, once upon a time He was a child, too.

First Big Holiday

(Luke 2:41, 42)

ONE BY one the happy years of childhood slipped away. There came a day when Jesus had His fifth birthday. Then His sixth, His seventh, His eighth. And every passing year He became more and more the joy and wonder of His mother's heart. Never had there been a little boy so good, so gentle, so friendly, so bright, and so thoughtful of the needs of others.

By the time He was 9, 10, 11, He must have been a wonderful help and comfort to His parents. He was always looking for ways to make life easier for them, mending this and fixing that and running quickly to do what they asked. And often His lovely voice filled the house with the melody of sacred songs.

At nighttime, after He had fallen asleep, I can see Mary sitting by His bedside marveling at the sweetness of His character as she thought of all the kind things He had said and done that day. Then she would think of Gabriel again, and what he had said to her: "He will be great and will be called the Son of the Most High."

"No wonder He is so dear and good and beautiful!" I can hear her saying to herself. "Surely someone so full of love, so utterly unselfish, must be the Son of God."

All through these early years Jesus learned more and more about the Holy Scriptures. After Mary had taught Him how to read, He began to study them Himself, and He asked her many questions about the meaning of texts that were not yet clear to Him.

He was especially interested in all that the prophets said about the coming of a little Boy who would grow up to be the

Deliverer of Israel and the Restorer of all that Adam and Eve had lost in Eden. Gradually He began to understand God's wonderful plan of salvation. Gradually, too, the truth dawned upon Him that He must be this Child of destiny.

Exactly when this thought first came to Him we do not know. But when it did, I am sure He became more serious as He tried to think His way through it all—what it would mean to Him and the kind of life He would have to live.

When He became 12 years old, Mary and Joseph began talking to Him about a trip to Jerusalem to celebrate the Passover.

There were three annual feasts that all the men of Israel were supposed to attend—Passover, Pentecost, and Tabernacles. The first was in the early spring, the second, seven weeks later, and the third was in the autumn, after the harvest. Everyone wasn't able to go to all of them, of course, but most people did their best to get to the Passover.

Since Jesus was now a youth—12 was the dividing line between childhood and youth in those days—Mary and Joseph felt that He should go with them this year. You can imagine how happy Jesus was when He was told about it. Nineteen hundred years ago, a trip to Jerusalem must have seemed very wonderful to a carpenter's son in Nazareth.

Can't you hear Jesus saying to Mary, "May I really go, Mother? Really? Do you mean it?"

Then they must have talked about all the things He would

see in Jerusalem: the Temple, Herod's palace, and all the old stores and houses. There would be priests offering sacrifices and Roman soldiers marching up and down the streets to keep order. And there would be all sorts of people, from far and near, crowding every nook and corner of the city.

The next few days were busy ones as Joseph tried to get his carpentry work done. Mary prepared food for the journey, and Jesus groomed the donkey and did what else He could to help get everything ready. Then they were off.

It was the first big holiday trip Jesus had taken, and He enjoyed every minute of it. When they reached the main road to Jerusalem, they found it thronged with people all going in the same direction. Jesus watched them with keenest interest, wondering, perhaps, whether they all understood why they were going to the Passover.

He understood, of course. Time and again He had talked

about the Passover with His mother. Now as He traveled toward the Holy City, He thought about that last night in Egypt, just before Moses had led Israel out to safety. This was when God had warned the people to sprinkle the blood of a lamb on the sides and tops of the doorframes of their homes, saying, "When I see the blood, I will pass over you."

The Passover was something very sacred to Jesus, bringing back memories of God's wonderful care for His people. But still there were questions in His mind. Why did God say a lamb should be killed? Why was the lamb's blood used in such a way? Could this be further proof that Messiah must suffer before He could save?

Surely someone in Jerusalem could tell Him. Maybe the priests, if they would listen to a boy. If He just got a chance, what a lot of questions He would ask them!

Teaching the Teachers

(Luke 2:42, 43, 46, 47)

AS MARY, Joseph, and Jesus drew near to Jerusalem the highway became more crowded than ever. Jesus had never seen so many people in all His life. Thousands upon thousands were moving into the city from all directions for the Passover services.

As He caught sight of the city and saw the Temple standing on Mount Moriah He was greatly stirred. Old Bible stories that His mother had taught Him from childhood suddenly took on new meaning.

How wonderful to be looking at the very place where Abraham offered up Isaac, where David defeated the Jebusites and Solomon reigned in all his glory! Here the prophets of God had spoken for 1,000 years and more!

Yes, and someday Messiah would come to this city. He would ride "on a colt, the foal of a donkey," [1] as Zechariah had prophesied. Jesus may have said to Himself, "Someday, in God's good time, I will ride along this road and through these very gates!"

Inside the city at last, the family was soon very busy. They had to find a place to stay, buy food, then go on to the Temple, where the first Passover services were about to begin.

Jesus watched everything with wide-open eyes, for it was all so new to Him. He wondered why there were so many poor people, so many beggars, so many sick, and His loving heart went out to them all.

When they arrived at the Temple, Jesus was surprised to find that it looked more like a cattle market than a place of worship. Merchants were selling cattle, sheep, lambs, and birds to the people who had come to worship. Moneychangers were noisily arguing with visitors about exchange rates.

"But why do they do it here?" I can hear Jesus saying to Mary. "It's not right, Mother! It's not right!"

"I know, dear," Mary may have said. "But they have done it so long that nobody thinks there's anything wrong about it."

"But the Scriptures say, 'My house will be called a house of prayer.' [2] It shouldn't be a marketplace like this!"

To a boy brought up as Jesus had been it must have been a terrible shock to find such things going on in the holy Temple. But it was only the first of many disappointments He suffered.

He saw rich people drop gold and silver coins into the offering box with a loud noise, then look around to make sure their gift had been noticed. Jesus didn't like that. He saw poor people made to wait just because they were poor, and He didn't like that either. Worse still was the formal way in which the sacrifices were offered. Most of the people were doing it because it was a custom, and not because, deep down in their hearts, they were sorry for their sins.

As the days slipped by, Jesus longed more and more to talk to some of the priests and ask them about these things and all the other questions He had wondered about for so long.

At last His chance came. There was a room in the Temple buildings where young people were taught by rabbis during the big feasts. While His parents were busy somewhere else, Jesus found His way here, and sitting down among other boys of His age, looked up at the bearded old teacher with rapt attention.

Never had He been so happy! This was what He had longed for! Pretty soon His hand shot up. "May I ask a question?" said this lad with bright eyes and open, earnest face.

"Certainly, my boy," the teacher said. "What is it?"

Then came that first question, which showed such a knowledge of the subject that the teacher was shocked.

I wish I knew what that question was, don't you? Somehow I feel sure that it had to do with the prophecies about the Messiah. The teacher may have said that Messiah would come and reign as a king in glorious splendor; and Jesus may have asked, "But what about the prophecy in Isaiah, 'He was pierced for our transgressions, he was crushed for our iniquities'?" [3]

As the rabbi answered, Jesus came back with another question and another, each one more pointed than the last. Other rabbis drifted in to see what was going on, and stayed to listen to this remarkable Child who knew the Holy Scriptures so well and seemed aware of hidden meanings these famous teachers had never thought about before.

After a while they began to ask Him questions.

"Where were you born?"

"In Bethlehem of Judea."

"Where do you live?"

"In Nazareth of Galilee."

"Where did you go to school?"

"I didn't go to school."

"Then how did you learn the Scriptures so well?"

"My mother taught Me."

Then they asked Him more questions to see how much He knew about the writings of patriarchs and prophets, and Jesus didn't miss one of them. So quick and right were His answers that they were all amazed. The Bible says that "everyone who heard him was amazed at his understanding and his answers."

Hour after hour they talked together like this. Nobody got tired or hungry. The Passover services came to an end, and the thousands of visitors began to go home. But the priests and rabbis stayed on with this young boy from Nazareth who had aroused their interest as no one else had done for a long time.

As for Jesus, He was enjoying Himself so much that it never dawned on Him that His parents might already be on the way to Galilee. But they were. And soon they would be hunting for Him all over Jerusalem.

---

[1] Zechariah 9:9.
[2] Isaiah 56:7.
[3] Isaiah 53:5.

PAINTING BY WILLIAM HUTCHINSON

After the Passover services had come to an end Jesus slipped away from His parents and went to the Temple to reason with the rabbis. They marveled at His knowledge of the Scriptures.

Lost Boy Found

(Luke 2:43-46, 48-50)

EXACTLY how far Joseph and Mary had gone on their way home when they missed Jesus, we will never know. The Bible says "they traveled on for a day," and that could have been no more than a dozen miles or so, with the narrow roads crowded with people returning to their homes from the Passover.

All this time they had been chatting pleasantly with friends, talking about the happenings of the past few days in Jerusalem. Most likely it was in the early evening, when they stopped to rest for the night, that they first noticed that Jesus wasn't with them. They had thought He was close behind them, but they had not bothered to make sure. Now, when they expected Him to come running to help them attend to the donkey and do other odd jobs as He always did, no Jesus came.

"Jesus!" they called anxiously, as they looked the crowd

over. "Where are You? We're waiting for You!" They felt sure He must be somewhere in that vast throng, perhaps talking with other boys of His age. But He wasn't.

"Je-sus! Je-sus!" they called again and again, but their voices were lost in the chatter of the people, the barking of dogs, the braying of donkeys, and the squeak and crunch of wagons going by.

After a while, when Jesus did not answer, Joseph and Mary began to get anxious. Now they started to look for Him in earnest. "We've lost our Son," they said to friends and strangers alike. "Have you seen Him anywhere?"

"Sorry, no," came the reply. "When did you last see Him?" they asked.

"Not since we were in Jerusalem. We thought He was right behind us."

"Too bad. Maybe you'd better go back."

Go back! All that way! At first Joseph and Mary felt annoyed. Why hadn't He kept up with them? But then they remembered how Herod had tried to take His life. Could He still be in danger? Had something happened to Him?

With fear gripping their hearts, they started back to Jerusalem. Anxiously they peered through the gathering darkness at everybody traveling in the opposite direction. But there was no sign of Him anywhere.

Passing through the city gates, they went back to the place where they had stayed. They hoped He might be there, waiting for them. But He wasn't.

They knocked on the doors of nearby houses. "Excuse us, please, but we've lost our Son. Have you seen Him? He's just 12 years old, and we brought Him here for the Passover."

"Sorry, no." It was the same everywhere. Nobody had seen Him. Nobody knew anything about Him.

For hours and hours they searched. "Where shall we try next?" I can hear Joseph saying.

"There's the Temple," Mary may well have said. "You know how He loved being there."

So they went to the Temple.

The great Passover crowds were gone and the usual quietness had settled down again. They saw a priest going by.

"Have you seen a boy about 12 years of age?" they asked him. "We can't find our Son, and we wondered if He might be here."

"Do you mean the boy from Nazareth?"

"Yes! That's right. We are from Nazareth. Do you know where He is?"

"Well, He was over there in the young people's room. Several of the rabbis have been talking to Him. Maybe He's there still."

Quickly Joseph and Mary hurried across the courtyard. They found the room and stood outside listening. They could hear a man asking a question. One of the rabbis, no doubt. Then another voice answered, clear, soft, musical, but very steady and sure. There was no mistaking it. It was *His* voice! Thank God they had found Him at last!

Opening the door, they saw an unforgettable sight. There was their precious Jesus "sitting among the teachers, listening to them and asking them questions."

Mary was so glad to see Him that she forgot all about the learned doctors and ran over to Him with outstretched arms. "Son," she said in tender rebuke, "why have you treated us like this? Your father and I have been anxiously searching for you."

Just as lovingly, Jesus answered, "Why were you searching for me? . . . Didn't you know I had to be in my Father's house?"

The meeting broke up, and the doctors began to leave. But some of them heard what Jesus said and wondered what He meant by "my Father's house." Hadn't He said His father was a carpenter? But Mary understood. She knew that Jesus was not thinking about Joseph, but God. And as she looked into His eyes she knew that He had found something here while talking with these leaders of Israel.

There was a new certainty in His voice. He was sure now that He must be the Messiah.

PART TWO STORY 6

The Carpenter's Son

(Luke 2:51, 52)

AS JOSEPH and Mary started off once more for Nazareth, this time with Jesus close beside them, they had much to talk about. Can't you hear Mary asking Jesus, "What did the teachers say to you, dear? And what did you say to them? Tell us all about it."

What Jesus told them we do not know, but He surely had a tale to tell about the rabbis and all the questions they had asked Him and that He had asked them. Don't you wish you could have listened? I do.

No doubt, as they journeyed on, Mary and Joseph told how they had missed Him that first night out of Jerusalem and how they had hunted for Him everywhere until they had found Him in the Temple.

I am sure they were very sorry that they had lost sight of their precious Son for so long. They hadn't meant to; they had just been too wrapped up in other things and other people. How careful we must be not to let anything or anybody crowd Him out of our thoughts! It is so easy to lose Him, so hard to find Him again.

A few days later they arrived in Nazareth, tired, but happy to be home again, safe and sound.

All that the Bible says about the next 18 years of Jesus' life is found in this one text: "Then he went down to Nazareth with them and was obedient to them. . . . And Jesus grew in wisdom and stature, and in favor with God and men."

Eighteen years in 27 words! Yet how much they tell!

He "continued to be under their authority" (NEB). This means He was obedient and courteous to His parents, even in His teens, when some boys and girls cause so much trouble.

He did what He was asked to do cheerfully and graciously, never grumbling or complaining. He often sang as He worked, and He found His greatest joy in making His parents happy, caring for their needs, and respecting their slightest wishes.

What a wonderful example He set before us all! If you want to be like Jesus, you must be kind, loving, and obedient to *your* parents, helping them all you can.

As the years went by, He "grew in wisdom." This means that He did not stop studying at 15 or 16, thinking He knew everything. He went on learning more and more—about the Bible, about nature, about people.

There were no high schools and universities then such as most young people of today can attend if they wish. There were no public libraries in His town, where He could go and borrow books on any subject, as you can. Yet by reading all He could find in the synagogue, by exploring the secrets of nature, by mixing with all sorts of people, and above all, by talking with God in prayer, He became wiser than anyone who ever lived on earth either before or after Him.

He also "grew in . . . stature." This means that He was not a weakling. He paid attention to His health. He ate well and got plenty of exercise. Knowing that He was to be the Messiah, He understood that He would need great strength to stand the strain. So He never let Himself begin bad habits of any kind.

No doubt other boys in Nazareth did many foolish things that weakened their bodies and spoiled their characters—just as smoking, drinking, and drugs damage young people today. But Jesus would have nothing to do with anything that would harm His mind or His body. His life was dedicated to a great purpose, as yours and mine should be.

Because of all this He "grew . . . in favor with God and men."

All heaven was watching this noble Youth. From the moment the angels had sung at His birth, they had watched over

Him everywhere He went. Just as they had rejoiced over the sweetest Baby ever born, so now they gloried in this grandest Youth who ever walked the earth.

And not only was heaven pleased with Him. For miles around Nazareth, He was respected by men, women, and children alike. They loved Him because He was so gentle, kind, and friendly. They loved Him because He was so clean, pure, and truthful. They loved Him because He was so unselfish, so sympathetic, so thoughtful of others.

In the carpenter's shop He put His best into every job that Joseph gave Him to do. And what a pity it is that not one thing He made has been kept for us to see! A baby's crib, perhaps, a doll's bed, an armchair, or a chest of drawers. If such a thing existed, made by Jesus' own hands, it would be worth a fortune; but it would also be the finest example of faultless work for boys and girls today. How square would be the saw cuts! How exact the corner joints! How smooth the surfaces! How invisible the joints! The finest cabinetmakers in the world would say, "This is the work of a master craftsman!"

Sometimes, perhaps when He was 18, 19, or 20, Jesus would wonder why He had to stay in a carpenter's shop so long.

PAINTING BY MANNING DE V. LEE

With the world waiting for the message He had to give, why waste time bending over a bench, planing wood, sharpening saws and chisels! But it was not time wasted. By striving always to do perfect work He was preparing Himself for the greater tasks ahead of Him.

In His heart He was sure He had come from heaven to earth to reveal God's love to men. And this meant showing love in all its beauty in the home, in the workshop, in the synagogue, along the city streets—anywhere, everywhere. It meant also setting an example of perfection in everything He did or said. He could never let one poor, unworthy piece of work come from His hands or let one unkind word fall from His lips.

What an example He set us! Today, 2,000 years later, He wants us to follow in His steps, to strive to live as He did. He will help us with every task He has asked us to do for Him. And as we learn to work hand in hand with Him we too will grow "in wisdom and stature, and in favor with God and men."

PART THREE

Stories of Jesus' Ministry

(Matthew 3:1-4:22; Mark 1:1-20; Luke 3:1-4:13; John 1:1-4:42)

Exciting News

(Luke 3:1, 2)

LIFE must have been much quieter for the young people of Nazareth long ago. They had no newspapers, radios, or TVs to tell them what was going on in the world around them. Except for a few old scrolls in the synagogue, there was little or nothing for them to read.

Wages were small, and week after week they worked in the fields or shops to earn enough money to buy their food and pay their taxes. Other than an occasional wedding or funeral, not many exciting things happened. Some believe that Joseph must have died about this time, for he is not mentioned again in the story of Jesus' life.

When Jesus had His twenty-first birthday, He was still just a carpenter, working at His bench day after day, making furniture or mending wagons or cart wheels for passing travelers. Twenty-two, 23, 24. Slowly the peaceful, carefree years passed by.

Spring, summer, autumn, winter, came and went, again and again. Harvest followed seedtime. Babies were born, and

← PAINTING BY RUSSELL HARLAN

Bidding His mother farewell Jesus went out from His quiet home at Nazareth to three and a half years of ministry, preaching to the poor, teaching the people, and healing the sick.

old people died. But still nothing important disturbed the quiet of Nazareth.

Sabbath after Sabbath Jesus and His mother walked along the quiet streets to the synagogue and listened to some rabbi reading from the Holy Scriptures. It must have seemed to them that life in this old village would go on like this forever.

Then one day a man arrived with an unusual story, which quickly spread from one end of town to the other. Stopping by the carpenter shop, he told Jesus about it.

Down by the Jordan River, he said, at a place called Bethany, a strange man had begun to preach. Hundreds of people were going out to listen to him, even from as far away as Jerusalem. His message was so powerful that the whole country was getting excited about it.

"What is his name?" Jesus must have asked.

"He calls himself John, and he says he is preparing the way for the coming of some great Person who is to become the Judge and Ruler of Israel."

"Does he tell the people to rebel against the Romans?"

"Oh, no. Many Roman soldiers listen to him too. He just tells everybody to repent and stop doing wrong, so that they will be ready to meet the Messiah [which means "Anointed One"] when He comes."

"And then?"

"Well, then he baptizes them—puts them right under the water to show that their sins have all been washed away."

"Are many being baptized?"

"Oh, yes, hundreds and hundreds. It's a wonderful sight. You ought to go and see it."

This was great news. And it must have been a solemn moment when Jesus told His mother about it. I can hear Him saying, "Mother, Cousin John has begun to preach. I must go to him. The time has come."

Mary understood. She had been afraid that something like this might happen someday. Now her mind went back to that time 30 years before, when Elizabeth had told her what the angel Gabriel had said about her baby John.

"He will be great in the sight of the Lord," he had said. "Many of the people of Israel will he bring back to the Lord their God. And he will go on before the Lord, in the spirit and power of Elijah, to turn the hearts of the fathers to their children and the disobedient to the wisdom of the righteous—to make ready a people prepared for the Lord."

The time must have arrived for Gabriel's words to come true. And if her own precious Jesus was really "the Son of the Most High," as Gabriel had said He was, He must be the One John was preaching about.

Tenderly they said goodbye, both knowing in their hearts that the happy days in Nazareth were gone for good. Then, clearing His bench for the last time and carefully putting away the tools He would never use again, Jesus closed the door of His carpenter shop and set out for the Jordan.

It was the parting of the ways for Him. Behind Him lay the precious memories of boyhood and youth, the pleasant work-days and happy Sabbaths around His old home, and the wonderful hours spent with His heavenly Father up on the mountainside and in the nearby fields and forests.

Ahead were days of toil and sorrow, of temptation and trial. The Messiah would be King someday, He knew, but He must die before He could reign. He would be "a man of sorrows, and familiar with suffering." * The Holy Scriptures said so. But He did not draw back. Now He would begin the wonderful ministry of preaching, teaching, and healing to which God had called Him.

Striding bravely down the steep mountain trail, He made His way to John—to Bethany, Gethsemane, and Calvary.

* Isaiah 53:3.

The Shining Light

(Matthew 3:1-10; Luke 3:3-15)

JESUS had no trouble finding John the Baptist. All the roads to the Jordan River were crowded with thousands of people going to listen to him. As Jesus mingled with the crowd He saw His cousin standing on a small knoll near the riverbank.

John was a striking figure. Instead of dressing in the flowing robes of the rich and learned, he wore clothes made of camel's hair, with "a leather belt around his waist." As he preached, his eyes seemed to flash fire, and his powerful voice boomed across the valley, imploring the people to turn from their sins and come back to God while there was still time.

What a preacher! High and low, rich and poor, were caught up with his message. No wonder Gabriel had said he would be like Elijah! He surely was. Just as Elijah had defied the prophets of Baal on Carmel, so John boldly rebuked the richest and most powerful men in Israel for their sins. Fearlessly he exposed the wickedness of Herod, just as Elijah had rebuked King Ahab. He seemed to be, as Jesus said afterward, "a lamp that burned and gave light."

Seeing some of the Pharisees and Sadducees in his congregation, he called them a "brood of vipers" and asked them, "Who warned you to flee from the coming wrath? Produce fruit in keeping with repentance."

Knowing what they were thinking, he added, "Do not think you can say to yourselves, 'We have Abraham as our father.' I tell you that out of these stones God can raise up children for Abraham."

Being children of Abraham wouldn't help them in the judgment if they had not walked with God as Abraham had. Having the most famous man who ever lived as their father wouldn't help them a bit if they were not sorry for their sins.

"The ax is already at the root of the trees," John cried, "and every tree that does not produce good fruit will be cut down and thrown into the fire."

This was a warning all could understand. Everybody in the crowd, at some time or other, had seen a barren tree cut down and burned. So they began asking themselves what sort of fruit their lives were bearing. Was it good or bad, sweet or sour, wholesome or rotten? They knew the answer.

As the preacher's fiery words burned into their hearts, it seemed as though God Himself were speaking to them. The "lamp that burned and gave light" was breaking through every barrier, revealing all the darkness, the meanness, the cruelty, in their hearts.

"What shall we do?" they began to cry. And John replied,

hitting hard at their selfishness, "The man with two tunics should share with him who has none, and the one who has food should do the same."

The tax collectors in the crowd cried out, "What should we do?" Knowing their greed, John answered, "Don't collect any more than you are required to."

Even some of the Roman soldiers who had come to listen out of idle curiosity were moved by John's earnest preaching. "And what should we do?" they asked. And John replied, "Don't extort money and don't accuse people falsely—be content with your pay."

Never had anyone had the courage to talk so plainly to the rich and the mighty as this remarkable man. And the amazing thing was that they took it from him and came back for more.

Hundreds began to confess their sins and, forming a long line, moved down to the river to ask the prophet to baptize them. Pharisees, Sadducees, tax collectors, and soldiers mingled with the common people as John dipped them one by one in the waters of the Jordan. Nothing like this had ever been seen in Israel before. Surely a great new day was dawning!

"Thank God!" the people said one to another after the meeting, as they sat around sharing their lunches as John had told them to do. "At last another prophet has come to us!"

"He must be Elijah, risen from the dead!" some said, while others whispered, "He could be the Messiah. He is just the man to deliver us from the Romans."

And Jesus, listening, wondered and waited.

A Voice From Heaven

(Matthew 3:13-17; John 1:19-28)

THAT whispered word spread like wildfire. "The Messiah!"

From group to group it swept until everybody in the crowd was looking at John with great hope. Perhaps this mighty preacher, who could move hearts so deeply that even Pharisees and Sadducees humbly asked for baptism, might be the very One Israel had been waiting for so long.

Then somebody told John, and he was shocked. "No, no!" he cried. "I am not the Christ. I am only His messenger, sent to prepare the way before Him."

"Are you Elijah, then?" someone asked.

"No, not Elijah," said John.

"Then who are you?"

"I am the voice of one calling in the desert, 'Make straight the way for the Lord.' "

"If you are not the Christ or Elijah," asked a Pharisee, "why are you baptizing people?"

" 'I baptize with water,' John replied, 'but among you

stands one you do not know. He is the one who comes after me, the thongs of whose sandals I am not worthy to untie.' "

"What does he mean?" the people must have asked. "Is the Messiah already here? Is He somewhere in this crowd?"

They began to look around. But they couldn't see anybody who looked like the Messiah they expected. Surely John must be mistaken. There was nobody here whose shoes he wasn't worthy to untie. It was all very strange. They wished John wouldn't be so mysterious sometimes.

While everybody was talking and wondering what John meant, a young Galilean about 30 years old began moving closer to the riverbank. Nobody took any special notice of Him. He was just one of the crowd going to be baptized.

Suddenly John looked up. As he caught sight of Jesus a strange look came over his face. Of all the hundreds of people who had come to him for baptism, he had never seen anyone like this. Purity, goodness, nobility, shone from His clear eyes and kindly face. There was something strangely Godlike about Him. Surely this must be the Messiah!

When Jesus asked for baptism, John refused. "Oh, no," he said. "You should baptize me."

But Jesus insisted. "Let it be so," He said. He wanted to "fulfil all righteousness." He had no sins to be washed away, but He wanted to set a perfect example before all who would follow Him. If He had not been baptized, others would have had an excuse for saying that they did not need to be baptized either; and Jesus knew that would not be good for them.

John at last agreed. Gently he lowered Jesus into the Jordan until the water covered Him completely. Then, just as carefully, he lifted Him again to His feet.

At that very moment something marvelous happened. The Bible says that as Jesus went up out of the water, "heaven was opened, and he saw the Spirit of God descending like a dove and lighting on him. And a voice from heaven said, 'This is my Son, whom I love; with him I am well pleased.' "

How very, very wonderful! Among all the jostling crowd, His Father had recognized Him, and called Him "my Son, whom I love"! From all His mother had told Him and from all His study of the Scriptures, Jesus had believed He must be the

M. deV. Lee

Son of God, sent to be the Saviour of the world. Now He was doubly sure, beyond all possibility of doubt.

All heaven had been waiting and watching for this moment, for this was the time when the precious Baby of Bethlehem, the noble Youth of Nazareth, would become "the Anointed One, the ruler" [1]—anointed by the Holy Spirit of God. And it had happened at the exact time foretold by Gabriel to Daniel long years before.

Now, after 30 years of preparation, of study, work, and worship, Jesus was ready to begin His ministry of love that had been planned for Him "from the creation of the world." [2]

How beautiful it was for His Father to tell Him on the day of His anointing, "This is my Son, whom I love; with him I am well pleased." Just to know that His Father loved Him and was pleased with Him must have meant more to Jesus than we can ever imagine.

You like your father to be pleased with you, don't you?

Of course you do. Jesus was made happy, too, by His Father's words of praise. New courage filled His heart. Now He could go on to meet anything that might happen to Him in the days ahead.

[1] Daniel 9:25.
[2] Revelation 13:8.

The Lamb of God

(John 1:29)

SEEING the glorious light on Jesus' head, and hearing the voice from heaven, John knew for sure that he had just baptized the Messiah. Now, pointing to Jesus, he said, "Look, the Lamb of God, who takes away the sin of the world!"

The people around must have wondered what he meant. How could any man be a "lamb"? How could this young Galilean, this carpenter of Nazareth, take away the sin of the world?

Even John himself may not have fully understood the words he had been led to speak. But Jesus did. His mind went back to the first time He had seen a lamb offered as a sacrifice in the Temple. He remembered, too, how lambs had been killed in all the homes of Israel just before the great deliverance from Egypt.

Each of these events was part of a pattern, and the pieces were fitting together one by one. More and more clearly He saw that He too must be offered as a sacrifice before He could fulfill

His purpose to take away sin from the world forever.

Moments later John began to baptize again, and the long line of men and women, boys and girls, moved slowly by as he lowered them one by one into the water. Few, if any, gave another thought to what the Baptist had said to Jesus. But because of what happened later on Calvary, those strange but wonderful words of his have lived on down the ages.

Today they are thought to be among the most beautiful

words ever spoken. Every time we look at a picture of Jesus, or think of Him hanging on the cross, we seem to hear John saying again, "Look, the Lamb of God, who takes away the sin of the world!"

Jesus was indeed God's precious Lamb, His one and only Son. Only very great love—love beyond our understanding—could have led Him to give this Lamb to die for us. But that is just what He did.

When Abraham and Isaac were climbing a mountain in Moriah, you remember, the boy said to his father, "The fire and wood are here, . . . but where is the lamb for the burnt offering?" Abraham replied, "God himself will provide the lamb, . . . my son." * A little while later he saw a ram caught by its horns in a thicket, and the boy's life was saved.

Now once more God had provided a Lamb, His own dear Son, so that the lives of many boys and girls could be saved. This dear Lamb was not to die yet, for the time had not come. But someday—in just a little while—He would pay the price of sin for everybody. This is what John meant when he said that Jesus would take away the sin of the world.

Sin, which is another name for disobeying God, brings death. God made this plain to Adam and Eve before they ate the forbidden fruit in the Garden of Eden. But they took no notice of what He said, and so they had to pay the penalty.

There was no way out, no way back to Eden and to the life they had lost, unless someone paid the penalty for them. And this is what Jesus came to do. Not only for Adam and Eve, but for you and me and everybody. By coming to this world as the Lamb of God and dying in our place, He made it possible for us

to live forever—just as Adam and Eve could have if they had never sinned.

But this is not the only way Jesus "takes away the sin of the world." Boys and girls who truly love Him and believe that He is the Son of God soon find out that they do not want to do anything bad anymore. Somehow the love of Jesus fills their hearts so much that they want to be as good, and kind, and true, and honest, as He was.

So Jesus, the Lamb of God, not only took upon Himself the penalty of sin but also broke the power of sin.

What a wonderful plan it was! And how beautifully simple! Jesus planned to love us out of sin! Someday, Jesus thought, if He gave us all His love, we would begin to love Him. Then we would long to be good, just to please Him. At last there would come a time in a wonderful earth made new when everybody would love Him and want to be like Him. Then nowhere in all the wide, wide world, would one little sin be found.

This was His hope and His dream; and you and I can help to make it come true by asking Him to take away sin from our hearts today.

---

* Genesis 22:7, 8.

Battle in the Wilderness

Matthew 4:1, 2; Luke 4:1, 2)

AFTER His baptism Jesus did not begin to teach and heal right away. Instead He disappeared, and nobody knew where He had gone. John kept on preaching, but Jesus went off by Himself, walking mile after mile into the wild, desolate country that borders the Jordan valley.

The Bible says, "Jesus, full of the Holy Spirit, returned from the Jordan and was led by the Spirit in the desert."

He wanted to be alone, away from the noisy crowds. He wanted to be able to think about all that had happened at His baptism. The memory of it was so very sacred He could not share His thoughts with anybody.

His Father had spoken to Him! He had called Him "my Son, whom I love." He had said He was well pleased with Him! What a glorious moment that had been!

Yes, and He could still feel the thrill that surged through

His whole being as the Spirit of God came upon Him. Now as He strode along, He was "full of the Holy Spirit." His every thought was holy. He had a single purpose—to do the will of His Father with all His heart and mind and soul.

Coming to a shady spot, perhaps under an overhanging rock, He rested and, lifting His eyes heavenward, talked with His Father. What a beautiful prayer that must have been! What a pity nobody was there to write it down so that we could know what He said!

Maybe He gave thanks for the divine watchcare that had been over Him from His birth in Bethlehem until now, for the happy, peaceful days in Nazareth, and especially for His mother's love. Then, as He thought of what it meant to be the Son of God, the Messiah of Israel, the Saviour of the world, how He must have prayed for wisdom and strength and courage to do all that His Father expected of Him!

He earnestly prayed that the peace and love of Heaven would fill His soul and flow out to others in deeds of kindness and mercy. "Help Me, dear Father," He may well have cried, "to let everybody see that God is love."

Hour after hour He prayed, scarcely noticing the passing of time. The sun set and rose again while He still talked with His Father. Day after day of sweet communion slipped by.

Wild animals found His hiding place, but they did not try to hurt Him. A desert rat came to sniff, a fox peered around a giant boulder, a falcon flew low down the canyon and perched on a nearby crag, but it was only to look and wonder. They seemed surprised to find their good Creator here.

Jesus had brought no food with Him, and there was none to be found in the desert. So He did not eat. But He was so deep in thought that He did not feel hungry until 40 days and 40 nights had passed.

Then He became aware that He was not alone in the desert. Somebody had followed Him. Somebody evil. Somebody who hated Him. The Bible tells us that after nearly six weeks of fasting, when His body was very weak, Satan began to tempt Him. Then followed the great battle between the Prince of light and the prince of darkness.

They had been together before in heaven when Satan was known as Lucifer and it had been necessary for Christ to cast him out because of his wickedness. They had met in the Garden of Eden after Satan had spoiled God's beautiful plan for this world by deceiving Adam and Eve. Now they met again in this lonely desert place, with Satan eager to destroy the Saviour before His ministry could begin.

Gabriel was not far away, and legions of good angels were ready to leap to Jesus' side if Satan should try to hurt Him at this time. But they stood aside and let the evil one speak to Jesus and deceive Him if he could.

How anxiously they must have watched this battle of minds and hearts, this contest of wits and words! How they wanted Jesus to win!

They knew how subtle Satan can be. After all, he had deceived millions in the past 4,000 years. How then could Jesus—so young, so weak, so hungry—stand against his wiles? How much of the wisdom of God had He stored up in His heart since His boyhood? Was it enough for this hour of temptation?

Thank God, it was.

Three Terrible Temptations

(Matthew 4:3-11)

HAVE you ever gone without food for one whole day? If so, how hungry did you feel? You don't need to tell me. I can guess.

Imagine having nothing to eat for *two* days, or even *three* days. Wouldn't that be awful! And if you had to go for a whole week without food, I am sure you would be ready to eat the hardest crusts you could find anywhere.

Think how Jesus must have felt after almost six weeks without food! How He lived all that time without any breakfast or lunch or supper I do not know. But He did. And it was then, when He was weakest, that Satan struck his first blow.

"If you are the Son of God," he whispered in a kindly voice, "tell these stones to become bread."

It sounded so innocent, as temptations so often do. Satan spoke as if he were just trying to be helpful. The ground where they stood was covered with stones, and if Jesus was really the Son of God, it would be perfectly easy for Him to make just one or two of them into bread. Nobody would know about it, and He would feel much better.

But Jesus saw through the devil's sly plot. He scented danger in that little "if." Making a stone into bread would mean that He had a doubt in His mind about His relation to God. And how could He doubt when God had openly claimed Him as His own Son? Jesus also saw that if He were to use His power just to benefit Himself, it would be a selfish act, and such a thing He could not and would not do.

He saw too, that if He were to do this once, He would do it again and again until the whole purpose for which He had come into the world would be spoiled. People would come to Him not to learn about God but to get free food and clothes and houses and money. It would be very easy for Him to gather a great following this way, but it would not be God's way.

So, terribly hungry though He was, He refused, saying to Satan, "It is written: 'Man does not live on bread alone, but on every word that comes from the mouth of God.' "

Now Satan led Him to Jerusalem, and they stood together on the highest part of the Temple. Looking down, Jesus saw that it was a long way to the ground. One false step and He would plunge onto the rocks below. Satan could easily have tried to push Him over, but he didn't. He had something worse in mind.

Quoting Scripture himself this time, to make this second temptation seem more innocent than the first, he said, "If you are the Son of God, . . . throw yourself down. For it is written: 'He will command his angels concerning you, and they will lift you up in their hands, so that you will not strike your foot against a stone.' "

How very proper it sounded! Jesus was to claim a Bible promise and act on it. Why not?

But there was that nasty "if" again, and Jesus did not like it. Of course He believed the promise, but He was not going to claim it for Himself just to put on a show for Satan's benefit. The power of God was not to be used for such a purpose or for taking an unnecessary risk. So He said to Satan, "Do not put the Lord your God to the test."

With His clear mind, Jesus saw an even deadlier danger in this temptation. Like the first, its chief purpose was to ruin His mission to the world. He saw that if He jumped and was miraculously saved from death, people would flock to Him as to a magician. They would point to Him as "the man who jumped from the Temple." He wanted no cheap advertisement. He had come to save people by love, not by

acrobatics and circus stunts. The devil's suggestion was opposed to every principle for which He stood. He refused to listen to it.

Defeated again, the devil tried a new approach. He led Jesus to a mountaintop. Here, looking north, south, east, and west, they could see many cities and villages below them. Satan went on to talk of the glories of Memphis and Damascus, of Athens, Corinth, and Rome. He showed Jesus "all the kingdoms of the world and their splendor. 'All this I will give you,' he said, 'if you will bow down and worship me.' "

The devil knew that Jesus planned to set up a kingdom and that He expected to do it the hard way, by sacrifice and suffering, persuasion and love. So he offered Him a kingdom the easy way. "You can have your kingdom now," he said, "and it won't cost you anything. Just kneel down and worship me, and it's all yours."

It was the easy way, but Jesus was not interested in setting up a kingdom like those of the world, full of vice and wickedness. His plan was far different. He wanted a kingdom in which everybody would be good and kind and unselfish. As for falling down before Satan for any cheap glory he could give, Jesus would have none of it. "Away from me, Satan!" He said sternly, "For it is written: 'Worship the Lord your God, and serve him only.' "

What a blessing His knowledge of the Scriptures proved to be! The right words came to His mind just when they were needed. In the same way, our study of the Bible will help us meet the devil's temptations today.

When Satan saw that he could make no headway at all and that Jesus could not be moved one little bit from His loyalty to God, he went away. And He will leave us too, when he sees that we are determined to be true to God, whatever the cost.

Then, the Bible says, "angels came and attended him." Anxiously they had watched every moment of this awful struggle. Would Jesus be able to stand against the devil's schemes? they had wondered. Would He win this dreadful battle with the prince of darkness?

Now that Jesus' victory was no longer in doubt, they pressed close to Him with gladness and in ways unknown to us brought Him food and comfort. How long He stayed there we do not know, but as His strength began to return He set out for home.

Now there was a new light in His eye, a new confidence in His step and in His bearing. He had won the fight with His greatest enemy. He had proved that the worst temptations can be met and conquered. Tested, tried, and triumphant, He returned to the Jordan, back to the cities and villages of Israel, to begin the great work He had come into the world to do.

First Disciples

(Matthew 4:17-22; Mark 1:14-20; Luke 4:14; John 1:29-49)

NOBODY can be sure, of course, but I like to think that Jesus came out of the desert singing. Perhaps He was still pale from His weeks of fasting, but the Bible says that He "returned to Galilee in the power of the Spirit."

He had just won a great victory over Satan. Angels had talked with Him and brought Him food. Forty days and nights alone with God had made heaven very near and real to Him and filled His heart with courage for the future.

Now, as He walked along the mountain trail, perhaps He sang aloud that old familiar psalm His mother had taught Him long ago, "Give thanks to the Lord, for he is good; his love endures forever." *

He had work to do, and He wanted to get started. The hour had come for His message to be given to the world, and there was no time to lose. He had business to do for His Father.

Who was the first to see Him and hear His voice as He came down at last onto the plain of Jordan? Nobody knows. It could have been a shepherd watching his sheep or a farmer's wife milking a cow. And of course it *could* have been a group of boys and girls playing in a field. Looking up, they may have wondered who this friendly Stranger could be who smiled at them, waved His hand, and said, "The kingdom of God is near."

Coming to the river, He may have found a weary traveler watering his donkey. To him, as to everybody else He met, He broke the good news about His coming kingdom. "The time has come," Jesus said. "The kingdom of God is near. Repent and believe the good news!"

"That's just how John the Baptist talks," the man may have said.

"Have you heard him preach?"

"Oh, yes. He's a great preacher. People are still crowding to hear him."

Jesus was anxious to see John again and to find out how he was getting along. Mingling with the crowd, He came nearer to where His cousin was standing.

Suddenly, as John caught sight of Him, he stopped speaking. Pointing right at Jesus, he said, as he had once before, "Look, the Lamb of God, who takes away the sin of the world!"

Then he added, "This is the one I meant when I said, 'A man who comes after me has surpassed me because he

M.deV.Lee

was before me.' . . . I saw the Spirit come down from heaven as a dove and remain on him. I would not have known him, except that the one who sent me to baptize with water told me, 'The man on whom you see the Spirit come down and remain is he who will baptize with the Holy Spirit.' I have seen and I testify that this is the Son of God."

The crowd stirred in amazement and expectation. For weeks John had been saying that the Messiah was on His way, coming very soon. Now he was pointing at a man right in the group around him and saying, "This is He; this is the Son of God!"

People surged forward to catch a glimpse of the man John had pointed out. They pushed and shoved and stepped on one another's toes. There was danger of a riot, and Jesus, not wishing to be a cause of trouble or the center of a mob scene, quietly moved away. Unable to find Him, the people gradually settled down to listen to John.

The next day Jesus came to hear John again. As He walked among the people the Baptist caught sight of Him and called out once more, "Look, the Lamb of God!"

This time two men who heard these strange words followed Jesus out of the crowd. One of them was Andrew, the other, most likely John—the same John who, years later, wrote the Gospel that bears his name. Both were fishermen from Bethsaida, on the Sea of Galilee.

Noticing that He was being followed, Jesus turned and spoke

to the two young men. "What do you want?" He asked.

"Rabbi," they said to Him, "where do you live?"

"Come and see," He said, leading the way to His humble dwelling.

Because it was nearly sunset, Jesus invited them both to stay with Him, and they did. That brief visit changed not only their lives but the lives of millions of others. Actually it was the first meeting of the Christian church!

What Jesus said to Andrew and John during those few precious hours they were together we do not know. No doubt they asked Him what the Baptist meant by calling Him "the Lamb of God," and Jesus told them about Himself and the kingdom of love He had come to set up.

Maybe they didn't understand all He said, but there was something about His voice and His manner that made them feel sure it all must be true. Jesus' eyes seemed to look right through them, as though He knew everything about them, all they had ever done or were going to do. In that one short evening He won them both. They were His first disciples.

The next morning, Andrew, in great excitement, hurried off to find his brother Simon. " 'We have found the Messiah,' (that is, the Christ)," he said. "Come and meet Him."

Simon, another fisherman, wondered what this was all about. Should he go or shouldn't he? But Andrew persuaded him and "brought him to Jesus."

Jesus gave him a smile of welcome and said, to the fisherman's amazement, "Your name is Simon, but from now on it will be Peter." And so it was. Everybody has called him Peter from that day to this.

They were by Galilee now, and the little fishing boats were bobbing about on the blue water. " 'Follow me,' Jesus said, 'and I will make you fishers of men.' At once they left their nets and followed him."

Soon others joined the little group. Jesus found Philip, and Philip found Nathanael, saying to him, "We have found the one Moses wrote about in the Law, and about whom the prophets also wrote—Jesus of Nazareth, the son of Joseph."

"Oh, no," said Nathanael, "I can't believe that. Can any good thing come out of Nazareth?"

"Come and see," said Philip, and Nathanael followed him.

Then a strange thing happened. When Jesus saw Nathanael coming toward Him, He said, "Here is a true Israelite, in whom there is nothing false."

"How do you know me?" asked Nathanael, astonished.

"Before Philip called you," said Jesus, "when you were under the fig tree, I saw you."

Nathanael was shocked. How could Jesus have seen him under the fig tree? It was impossible. And yet, perhaps—"Rabbi," he cried, as light dawned upon his mind, "You are the Son of God; you are the King of Israel."

---

* Psalm 106:1.

Jesus Begins to Preach

(Luke 4:14, 15, 22, 32)

SETTING out with His little group of disciples, Jesus went from village to village in Galilee, telling over and over again the good news of His kingdom.

Everywhere He went He found that John had prepared the way for Him. Almost everybody was interested in what He had to say. They wanted to know more. They loved the simple, gentle, confident way He talked about the things of God. And they were thrilled by His knowledge of the Holy Scriptures. Whenever He quoted passages from the books of the prophets, they seemed alive with new meaning.

At first He was invited to speak in the synagogues, and the people crowded in to hear Him. Never had they listened to such wonderful preaching. The Bible says that they "were amazed at the gracious words that came from his lips."

Some people, of course, didn't like Him. They said He was just another rabble rouser trying to stir up the Jews against the Romans. But nobody could listen to Him for long without knowing this wasn't true, for His mission was peace.

Jesus made it as plain as He could that His kingdom was quite different from any other kingdom anybody had ever heard of. It was a kingdom of love, and anyone could belong to it any time he really wanted to. No war, no fighting, was needed to set up this kingdom, and the price of admission was a wish and a prayer—a wholehearted wish to be good and a sincere prayer of repentance and trust.

As for the Romans, there was no need to worry about them. Just love them, said Jesus, and everything would turn out fine. If the Romans order you to carry a load one mile, carry it two miles. If they take away your coat, offer them your shirt too. The toughest tyrant would soon soften if treated like that.

Someday, said Jesus, all the kingdoms of the world would pass away and God's kingdom of love would fill the earth. Paradise would be restored. Those who had let the love of God flood their hearts would find their way to the long-lost Garden of Eden.

In that day there would be no more hatred or strife.

Everybody would love everybody else. Kindness, gentleness, sympathy, would have driven out everything hateful and ugly.

Such teaching was so new and beautiful that the people drank it up. Synagogues that had been half empty for years suddenly became filled to overflowing with eager listeners.

Soon word spread everywhere that another great preacher had arrived, more wonderful even than John. Groups gathered around Him on the streets, asking questions and marveling at the wisdom of His answers.

They were amazed that He knew so much, in spite of the fact that He had never been to one of the schools of the rabbis. But best of all, they loved the way He took a personal interest in everybody. No matter who talked to Him—man, woman, or child—He had the same kindly smile and gracious word for each one. He knew just what to say to make everyone feel better. After being near Him just a little while, the people went away with a glow in their hearts.

No wonder the Bible says, "They were amazed at his teaching, because his message had authority."

Wedding Surprise

(John 2:1-11)

BY THIS time Jesus had been away from home many weeks. Now as He came close to Nazareth again, I am sure He thought about visiting the familiar old places once more. But instead of Nazareth, He was going to Cana, just six miles (10 kilometers) or so east of Nazareth, where He and His disciples had been invited to a wedding.

Jesus and His little band of followers climbed the steep, winding road from the lake to the little town. People wearing their best clothes were gathering around one of the houses. Oxcarts were parked along the street, and donkeys were tethered here and there.

"Looks as though everyone is here already," I can hear Peter saying. "What a lot of guests! Wonder if there are any here we know."

Just then Jesus caught sight of Mary, for she was at the wedding. "Mother!" He cried, greeting her with gladness.

How happy they must have been to meet again, though Mary noticed at once how He had changed. He looked older and thinner, but He was still her own dear Son.

"Meet my friends," I am sure Jesus said, introducing Andrew, Peter, John, Philip, and Nathanael.

"Come in! And welcome!" said Mary.

So Jesus and His friends sat down among the other guests.

They were probably strangers to some. "That's Mary's Son," whispered one guest, nodding in the direction of Jesus. "I hear He's become quite a preacher."

"Yes," said another. "Some say He preaches even better than John the Baptist."

"Maybe He will speak in our synagogue someday. We must get the rabbi to ask Him."

"Is it true John the Baptist said He is the Messiah?"

"That's what I heard; but I never thought the Messiah would look like that. Isn't the Messiah coming as a king?"

So the guests may have talked as they ate the good things provided for them at the wedding banquet. And Jesus, always friendly, chatted with those around Him, letting them see that He was glad to share their happiness.

Partway through the dinner Mary came over to where Jesus was sitting and whispered, "They have no more wine." She looked worried, and no wonder! This was serious—just as though your mother found that the punch was gone halfway through your birthday party.

For years Mary had counted on Jesus to help her out of difficulties, and He had never failed her. Now, motherlike, she turned to Him again. And she was so sure that He would know what to do that she said to the servants, "Whatever He says to you, do it."

Pointing to six large stone jars standing near the door, Jesus said, "Fill the jars with water."

The servants looked at the six jars and back again to Jesus. "What can He mean?" they wondered. "Doesn't He understand that it's wine, not water, that's wanted?"

But Mary had told them to obey, so they did. After they had gone to the well and filled the six big jars to the brim, Jesus told them to pour some out and carry it to the man in charge of the feast. This must have seemed a very strange thing for Him to say.

The servants probably wondered whether or not they should do it. What would the master of the banquet think if they turned up with a jug of water!

But again they obeyed, and something wonderful happened. As they tipped up one of the water jars, they noticed that the water had changed color.

"Look!" they cried. "It isn't water! It's wine!"

They tasted it to make sure it was all right, and their eyes opened wide! What wine this was!

Amazed and happy, they carried it to the man in charge and poured some into his cup. He tasted it, and *his* face lighted up. Never had he tasted such wine as this.

Calling the bridegroom, he asked him why he had kept the best wine till the last. But the bridegroom, astonished, wondered what the man was talking about. He hadn't kept any wine at all. He had thought it was all gone. Where had this wine come from? Who had brought it? Wine like this wasn't to be found anywhere in Galilee.

Soon all the guests were holding up their cups for some of this delicious wine and asking the same questions about it. But nobody could answer them. That is, not until the servants began to talk.

Then the guests crowded around the six stone water jars. "You really filled these with water?" they asked.

"Yes. At the well."

"And you put nothing else in them?"

"Nothing."

"And when you poured out the water, it had turned to wine?"

"That's the way it was. We saw it with our own eyes."

"A miracle!" cried everybody. "A miracle!"

And so it was. The Bible says, "This, the first of his miraculous signs, Jesus performed at Cana in Galilee. He thus revealed his glory, and his disciples put their faith in him."

Yet it was no miracle to Jesus. It was no more difficult for Him to turn water into wine in a water jar than to do it in a grapevine. He was just beginning to reveal His power as the Son of God.

The Temple Cleansed

(John 2:12-23)

RIGHT after the wedding at Cana, Jesus went to Capernaum with "his mother and brothers and his disciples." This meant a journey of 17 miles (27 kilometers) or so down the steep mountain road to the lake. But Jesus did not stay there long. In a few days He started for Jerusalem.

It was Passover time again—the first since His Father had openly declared Him to be the Son of God—and He felt He should spend it in the Holy City. This year, of all years, He must go there and let the great crowds know that the Messiah was among them.

How many of His disciples traveled with Him on this trip we do not know. A few, at least, went along, and the unhurried hours they spent together with their Master were precious. Jesus may have explained to them the true meaning of the Passover service and why so many lambs had to be slain on that long-ago night in Egypt before Israel escaped to the Promised Land. And He may have told them how the Lamb of God must someday be killed so that the world could be delivered from the power of sin. Then all who sprinkle the blood of God's Lamb on the doorposts of their hearts will be saved in His kingdom.

On that long walk to Jerusalem they mingled with hundreds of other pilgrims who were going the same way. Many were weary and troubled, but somehow everyone felt better as Jesus passed by. He always seemed to know the right words to say to cheer people up.

News of the miracle in Cana of Galilee had already spread far and wide, and every now and then someone would point to Jesus as the man who had turned water into wine. But soon people were talking about other miracles of His, for every time He touched the sick, they became well again.

By the time Jesus and His little party reached Jerusalem, many more people had come to love Him for His gracious words and kindly deeds. The Bible says that "while he was in Jerusalem at the Passover Feast, many people saw the miraculous signs he was doing and believed in his name."

As He came close to the Temple His face, which had looked so gentle as He had mingled with the common people, became stern. His keen ears had caught the noise of the market in the outer court. He could hear the lowing of cattle, the bleating of sheep, the shouts of excited merchants, and the loud arguments at the tables of the money changers. What bedlam!

As a boy of 12, Jesus had heard this same noise and had wished He could do something about driving these worldly people out of this holy place, but it was too soon then. Now the time had come for Him to show people the truth about the Temple services and the holiness of God. This was why He had come into the world, and what better time to begin than now?

Gathering up a few strands of cords that were lying around, Jesus twisted them together in the form of a whip. Then, lifting this in His right hand, He advanced in the power of the Spirit toward the money changers and merchants.

"Get these out of here!" He cried to those who were selling doves. "How dare you turn my Father's house into a market!"

At first no one took any notice of Him. There was so much clamor, so much confusion. So Jesus strode toward one of the money changers and tipped up his table, scattering the money all over the place.

Furious, the man leaped to his feet, ready to fight the one who had dared to do this to his property. But as he looked at Jesus and saw the glory of God on His face, he fled in terror. Now another table was overturned, and another, and another, as Jesus, utterly fearless, drove everybody before Him. Frightened cattle began to run too.

What a scene that was! Not one of those hardened merchants dared to defy Him. With their sheep and cattle, they stampeded toward the Temple gates to get away from this Man with the blazing eyes.

At last the Temple courtyard was quiet, and Jesus was left alone with His followers. Thousands of shekels lay all over the place with nobody to pick them up. It was a strange beginning to Jesus' ministry in the capital of Israel, but He could not have chosen a better way to let the whole country know that the Messiah had arrived.

A few minutes after the last table had been overturned and the last shekel had stopped rolling across the pavement, all Jerusalem was talking about what had happened in the Temple. How the people loved it! All their lives they had hoped that someday somebody would have the courage to do just this! Now Somebody *had* done it, and those mean, cheating merchants and money changers had run from Him. It seemed too good to be true!

Of course everybody began to ask who was so brave as to run this crowd of robbers out of the Temple. Some said that it was a Galilean, a carpenter from Nazareth. Others said it was the man who turned water into wine at Cana, and still others declared it was the very same person whom John the Baptist had called "the Lamb of God, who takes away the sin of the world."

Then hope began to rise as people asked one another, "Could this be the Messiah, the Saviour of Israel?"

Midnight Visitor

(John 3:1-17)

AFTER Jesus left the Temple court on that never-to-be-forgotten afternoon, the merchants and the money changers probably came right back, picked up their money, and started all over again.

But they were angry, as you can imagine. Their pride had been hurt. Everybody was laughing at them for running away from the gentle Carpenter of Nazareth. They vowed to get even with Him someday.

The priests were upset too. They didn't like the way this young reformer from the country had done what they should have done long ago.

But there were some among the leading people of Jerusalem who believed Jesus might be right. They had listened as He talked to the people, and they liked what He said to them. One of them, whose name was Nicodemus, decided to have a private talk with Jesus to find out more about Him.

But where was Jesus? Nobody seemed to know. Then

someone said He often went to the Mount of Olives in the evening to rest and pray. Nicodemus decided to follow Him there.

Waiting until it was dark so none of his friends would see where he was going, this famous ruler wrapped his cloak around him and set out into the night. How he found Jesus we do not know, but he did. And there in the moonlight, looking down on the sleeping city, they talked about the kingdom of God.

"Rabbi," said Nicodemus, "we know you are a teacher who has come from God. For no one could perform the miraculous signs you are doing if God were not with him."

Jesus was pleased to hear these gracious words from such an important man, and oh, how He wanted to help him understand the truth about His kingdom of love! "No one can see the kingdom of God," He said, "unless he is born again."

Nicodemus looked puzzled. "How can a man be born when he is old?" he asked.

Jesus must have smiled at this, for of course He was not

talking about the birth of a baby, but about what happens in the heart when the Holy Spirit comes into it. The change is so complete it's like being born again.

Jesus tried to explain. Pointing to the trees that were swaying gently in the cool night breeze, He said, "You know the wind is blowing because you can hear the rustling of the leaves, but you can't tell where the wind comes from or where it goes. That is how it is with those who are born of the Spirit."

He wanted Nicodemus to know that the Holy Spirit comes into any heart that is open to Him. Nobody can understand exactly how it happens, but everybody can see the results. Boys and girls who have the Holy Spirit in their hearts are kind and true and gentle. They love good and hate evil.

This was all new to Nicodemus. Famous though he was for his wisdom, he still didn't understand this very simple truth. "How can this be?" he asked.

"Are you a teacher of Israel," said Jesus, "and yet you still don't understand this?"

Then Jesus went on to tell more about how hearts and lives can be changed by the power of God. First He reminded Nicodemus of the time when Moses put a bronze serpent on a pole and everybody who looked at it was cured of snake bite. Then He said, "Just as Moses lifted up the snake in the desert, so the Son of Man must be lifted up, that everyone who believes in him may have eternal life."

Just one look at the Son of man will heal anyone of the bite of the great serpent Satan and make him whole again.

Nicodemus did not answer. He was too puzzled by these strangely moving words. Who was this "Son of Man"? he wondered. Could it be the Carpenter Himself?

Then Jesus spoke again, bringing to this earnest seeker after truth the most beautiful message that ever fell on human ears: "God so loved the world that he gave his one and only Son, that whoever believes in him shall not perish but have eternal life.

RUSSELL HARLAN, ARTIST

"For God did not send his Son into the world to condemn the world, but to save the world through him."

Though Jesus said this to just one man on a dark and silent hillside long ago, these precious words have spread around the world as though broadcast from some powerful radio station. Millions upon millions have heard them and been moved to tears by them. They have come down across the ages in all their beauty and power.

And why? Because they are the very heart of the gospel—that message of love that Jesus came from heaven to bring to the world. They tell how anybody, anywhere—boy or girl, man or woman—may enter the kingdom of God and live happily forever and ever.

And what is the secret? Just this: Believe Jesus loves you. That's all. Nothing else. Nothing to buy. Nothing to pay. Nothing to do but this. How simple! How beautifully, wonderfully simple!

Do you believe Jesus loves you? Really? Truly?

Then the kingdom is yours, now and always.

Sudden Harvest

(John 4:1-35)

AFTER the Passover Jesus stayed awhile in Judea, teaching and healing the people. Then with His disciples, He turned northward again toward Galilee.

On the way they stopped at a city called Sychar, which belonged to the Samaritans. These people, you remember, were descended from the strangers whom the king of Assyria brought into Palestine when he took the Israelites into captivity. Having lived here for hundreds of years, they felt that the country belonged to them just as much as to the Jews. But the Jews hated them and would have nothing to do with them.

While His disciples went into Sychar to buy food, Jesus, weary from the day's journey, sat down by a well. It was called Jacob's well because people believed Jacob had dug it when he passed this way.

Just then a Samaritan woman carrying a water jar walked up. Setting down her jar, she lowered a bucket into the water.

As she hauled it up again, Jesus spoke to her. "Will you give me a drink?" He asked.

The woman looked at Him in astonishment. "Why are you, a Jew, asking a Samaritan for a drink? The Jews don't deal with the Samaritans."

But there were no national barriers in His heart. He loved everybody, no matter where he was born. "If you knew who asked you for a drink," Jesus said, "you would have asked *Him* for a drink, and He would have given you living water."

"You don't have a bucket and the well is deep," said the woman. "Where do you keep this living water? Are you greater than our father Jacob, who gave us this well?"

Jesus answered in words that will live forever, "Everyone who drinks this water will be thirsty again, but whoever drinks the water I give him will never thirst. Indeed, the water I give him will become in him a spring of water welling up to eternal life."

The woman caught the meaning of the beautiful words, especially that "whoever." She saw that it included even her, a Samaritan.

"Sir," she cried, "give me this water so that I won't get thirsty and have to keep coming here to draw water."

Jesus smiled at her eagerness, but He had a lesson to teach her. "Go, call your husband and come back," He said.

The woman hung her head and said, "I have no husband."

"You have spoken the truth," said Jesus. "You have had

PAINTING BY KREIGH COLLINS

When the woman at Jacob's well realized that Jesus loved everybody, even the Samaritans, she eagerly requested that He give her to drink of the living water He had promised her.

five husbands, and the man you have now is not your husband."

The woman's eyes opened wide in amazement. How did this stranger know so much about her? "You must be a prophet!" she whispered.

Then she tried to change the subject by talking about the proper place for people to worship—whether it should be Jerusalem or Samaria. But Jesus kept bringing her back to the great truths of His kingdom.

"God is spirit," He said to her, "and his worshipers must worship in spirit and in truth." In other words, the place doesn't matter. Anyone, Jew or Samaritan, may worship God anywhere. What matters is the spirit in which one worships.

Somehow the conversation turned to the coming of the Messiah. "I know . . . [He] is coming," she said.

"When he comes, he will explain everything to us."

She was close to the kingdom now. So very close! And Jesus longed to bring her in. "I who speak to you am he," He said quietly.

What she said in reply we do not know, for at that moment the disciples returned with the food they had bought. They were amazed to find Him talking to a woman—and such a woman! Didn't He know she was a Samaritan? Didn't He know that she was living a very wicked life? But they didn't say what they thought.

"Rabbi, eat something," they said, spreading out the supper before Him.

But He couldn't eat. He was thinking about that poor woman and how near she had come to understanding the truth about Himself and His kingdom. He could still see her running back to the city as fast as she could, and He knew what would happen next.

Then He surprised His disciples by saying, "Do you not say, 'Four months more and then the harvest'? I tell you, open your eyes and look at the fields! They are ripe for harvest."

What could He mean? they wondered. Of course there were four months before the harvest, but what did that have to do with their supper? And how could there be a harvest to gather now?

Then they saw it. Coming out of the city gates was a crowd of excited people—men and women, boys and girls. They were running toward the well. In the crowd was the woman who had been with Jesus just a little while before. At the top of her voice she was shouting, "Come, see a man who told me everything I ever did. Could this be the Christ?"

What a harvest that was! and how quickly the seed had sprouted! It had not taken four months to gather this rich fruit—it had just taken a four-minute talk with Jesus.

On and on the people came, eager to meet the Messiah and hear His message for themselves—a harvest of Samaritans for His kingdom of love!

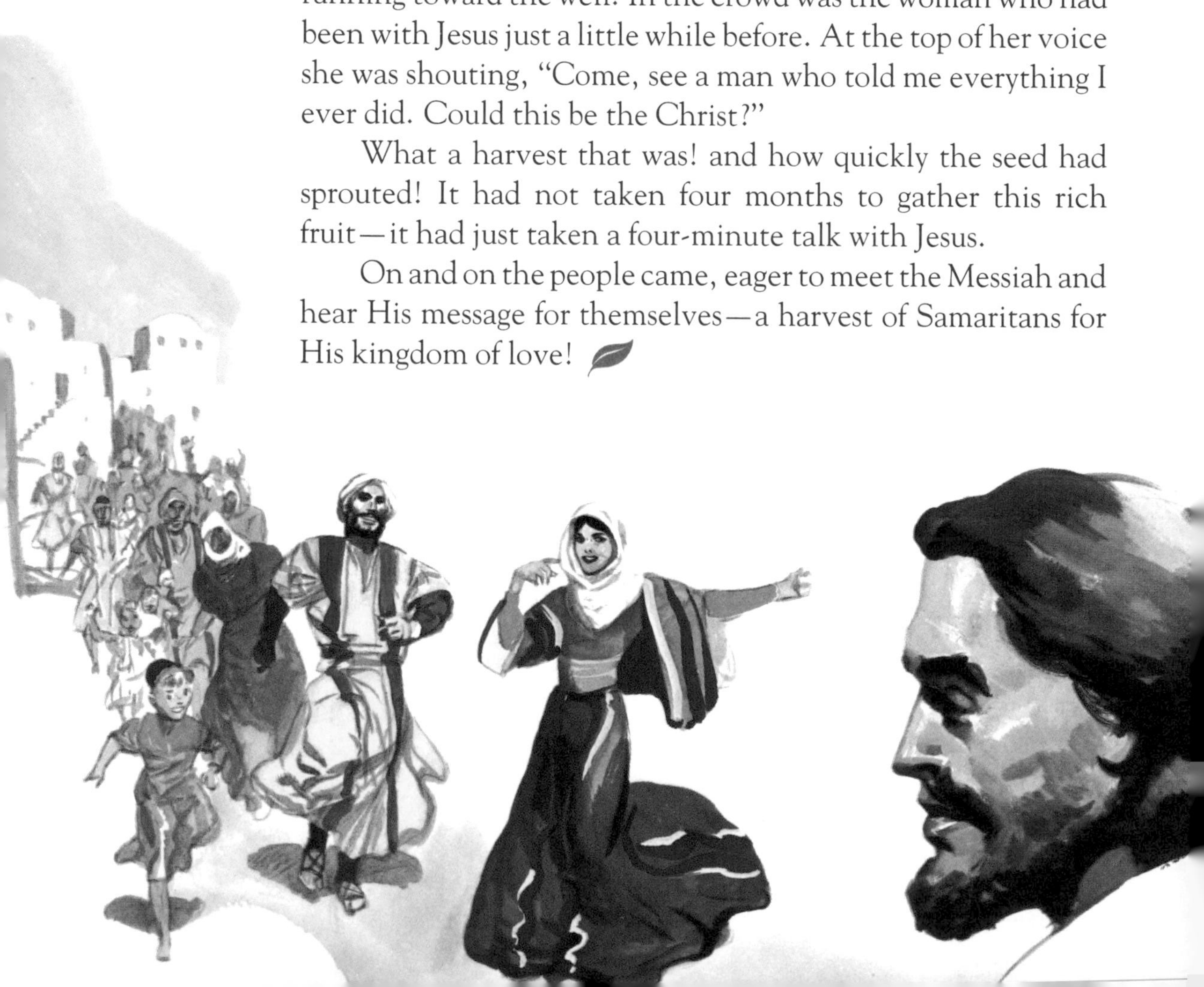

PART FOUR

Stories of Jesus' Miracles

(Matthew 4:23-25; 8:5-34; Mark 1:21-2:12; 4:35-5:20; Luke 4:14-5:11; 7:1-17; 8:22-40; John 4:43-54)

Daddy's Prayer Answered

(John 4:39-53)

SOON dozens of Samaritans were crowding around Jesus. Boys and girls pressed close to Him, while some struggled for a seat on the wall around the well. Could this stranger really be the Messiah? they wondered.

As Jesus talked about His kingdom of love they listened with growing eagerness. Never had they heard anybody speak like this. This Jesus of Nazareth was so kind, so gentle and understanding. He seemed to know everything about everybody.

Every boy thought He was talking to *him*. Every girl was sure He was talking to *her*. And the things He said were so simple that even the youngest knew what He was talking about. His words were so beautiful they seemed like living water bubbling up out of Jacob's well.

When at last Jesus said that maybe it was time to go everybody cried, "Oh, no, don't go! Stay and tell us more!"

So Jesus stayed. When darkness fell, the people took Him back to their village and gave Him the best room they could

← PAINTING BY KREIGH COLLINS

As Jesus talked about His kingdom of love, the children listened with growing eagerness, for every boy thought He was talking to him, and every girl was sure He was talking to her.

find. All the next day and the next He remained with them. No doubt He went from home to home, comforting the sad and making everybody feel better. By the time He left the village, there probably wasn't a single sick person in Sychar.

At last, when Jesus had to leave, tears filled many eyes. Nobody wanted Him to go. The Bible says that "many of the Samaritans . . . believed in him." Turning to the woman who had first told them about Jesus, they said, "We no longer believe just because of what you said; now we have heard for ourselves, and we know that this man really is the Savior of the world."

Traveling on northward, Jesus came once more to Cana of Galilee, where only a little while before, He had turned water into wine at the wedding banquet. Here He was given a hero's welcome. News of what had happened in Jerusalem had already reached the little city.

Everybody was thrilled at the story of how He had overturned the tables of the money changers and driven the greedy merchants out of the Temple. It was almost too good to be true that one of them, a Galilean, had had the courage to do such a thing!

Then, too, rumors were flying everywhere about the way Jesus had been healing people of all kinds of sicknesses. The Carpenter of Nazareth not only had turned water into wine but had given the blind their sight and the deaf their hearing! So now the people of Cana crowded around Him, as the villagers of Sychar had done.

About one o'clock in the afternoon, as they stood in the

market place listening to Jesus, a well-dressed man, evidently in a big hurry, started to push his way through the crowd. His clothes were dusty, for he had just ridden the 17 miles (27 kilometers) from Capernaum as fast as he could.

"Excuse me, please," the royal official was saying, "but I must get through to Him at once. It's very urgent."

The crowd opened to let him through.

"Come and heal my son," he cried to Jesus, "for he is close to death."

"Unless you people see miraculous signs and wonders," said Jesus tenderly, "you will never believe."

"Sir," begged the desperate man, "come down before my child dies!" How this daddy loved his little boy!

Jesus understood. "You may go," he said to the anxious man. "Your son will live."

Maybe it was the way Jesus said it or perhaps the look in His

eyes or the smile on His face. Whatever it was, the royal official knew that what He had said was true. He believed the word of Jesus and stopped worrying about his boy, as much as he loved him. To prove his faith he stayed in Cana with Jesus the rest of the day, even though his hometown was just a four-hour journey away.

The next day this royal official started out for Capernaum. On the way he met some of his servants coming up the hill. Their happy faces told him that they had good news. "Your son is well!" they cried eagerly.

"I know," said the royal official. "But, tell me, when did he begin to get better?"

"At one o'clock yesterday," they said, "the fever left him."

"One o'clock!" murmured the royal official. "One o'clock!" that was the very moment Jesus had said, "Your son will live." How very, very wonderful! He could hardly wait to get home to see his son and tell him what Jesus had done for him.

The Bible says that not only did he himself believe in Jesus, but "all his household" as well.

Madman in Church

(Mark 1:21-28)

THE SYNAGOGUE in Capernaum was packed. News had spread that Jesus was going to be there this Sabbath, and everybody in town had come to see and hear Him.

Some were there for the usual morning service, but most of those present had come to see the Man who had turned water into wine, healed the sick, and driven the merchants out of the Temple in Jerusalem.

When Jesus began to speak, a hush fell upon the crowd. All eyes were fixed on this wonderful new Preacher who seemed to have taken the place of John the Baptist. Unfortunately, John was now in prison.

"The time has come," said Jesus, breaking the silence. "The kingdom of God is near. Repent and believe the good news!"

With the ease and simplicity of a great teacher He showed from the Holy Scriptures that the hour had come for the Messiah to appear. The time prophecy that Gabriel had revealed to

Daniel was fulfilled. The Deliverer God had promised was with them. The woman's Offspring, promised to Eve in the Garden of Eden, was here to crush the snake's head. The Child of destiny, promised by the prophet Isaiah, had been born. He had grown up among them and now was ready to do the work God had given Him to do.

As Jesus spoke of how He had come to build a kingdom of goodness, peace, and love—a kingdom to which anybody, anywhere, could belong—the people listened intently. They "were amazed at his teaching, because he taught them as one who had authority, not as the teachers of the law."

Suddenly, perhaps as He was saying that anyone who wanted victory over evil could have it for the asking, a terrible shriek rent the air. All eyes turned to see what was the matter. They saw a madman in the synagogue, his eyes wild, his face twisted in pain. Men tried to lead him out, but he beat them off.

"Leave us alone!" he cried to Jesus. "What do you want with us, Jesus of Nazareth? Have you come to destroy us? I know who you are—the Holy One of God."

Jesus knew that this poor man was possessed by an evil spirit. One of Satan's evil angels was in control of his mind, making him behave like this.

Speaking to the evil spirit, Jesus said in a voice of command, "Be quiet! Come out of him!"

Suddenly the man let out another terrible cry. Then he staggered and fell. But it was the evil spirit's last struggle. In a moment it left him.

The man was now in his right mind. Weakly he looked up into the face of Jesus, pouring out his thanks.

The synagogue service was forgotten. Faced by this new wonder, the people could do nothing but talk. With their own eyes they had seen a madman healed! With their own ears they had heard the Carpenter of Nazareth give orders to an evil spirit, and the evil spirit had obeyed Him!

This was the most wonderful thing that had ever happened in Capernaum! The Bible says that "the people were all so amazed that they asked each other, 'What is this? A new teaching—and with authority! He even gives orders to evil spirits and they obey him.' "

Rushing from the synagogue, they hurried everywhere with the wonderful story. And the news of Jesus "spread quickly over the whole region of Galilee."

Flood Tide of Love

(Matthew 4:23-25; 8:14-17; Luke 4:38-41)

FROM this moment on it seemed as though a flood tide of love was being poured from heaven on the people of Galilee.

Jesus had come from heaven to earth to let everybody know that God is love, and now He went about this work by doing one kindly deed after another. Not only did He talk about God's love but He proved it by healing the people of all their sicknesses, great and small. Often after He had passed through a city or village there wasn't even one sick baby left in any home.

For a little while, at least, everyone was well and happy and full of hope. Boys and girls felt the warmth of His love. Yet He was just as thoughtful of the oldest grandpas and grandmas who came to hear Him.

Opening the floodgates of love kept Him busy every moment. The Bible says that "Jesus went throughout Galilee, teaching in their synagogues, preaching the good news of the kingdom, and healing every disease and sickness among the people."

Those who were well "brought to him all who were ill with various diseases, those suffering severe pain, the demon-possessed, those having seizures, and the paralyzed, and he healed them."

In homes all over Palestine children were talking about Him, saying, "If only we could take Mother to see this wonderful Man, perhaps she would get well again. Perhaps He could do something for her dreadful headaches. And Dad, poor old Dad, with his backache and that sore on his leg—perhaps he could be cured too. Somehow we must take them both to the Great Healer."

In thousands of homes children and older people were talking like this, wondering how they could find Jesus, then going with members of their families who were sick to meet Him. "Large crowds from Galilee, the Decapolis, Jerusalem, Judea and the region across the Jordan followed him."

No wonder! Wouldn't you have gone to see Him too if you had lived in those days? Of course you would. And especially if you had a toothache, or a bad cold, or cancer, or some other disease.

The sick—some hobbling along alone, some riding on donkeys, some carried by friends—came to Him from all directions and great distances, as if drawn by some powerful magnet. In His presence their groaning stopped; their cries of agony were stilled.

As news about the great Teacher and Healer spread farther and farther, more and more thousands came to Him. In His wonderful love "he . . . healed all the sick." He didn't stop to ask what race or nation they belonged to, or how much money they had, or how sinful they were. If they needed help and believed that He could give it to them, their wish was granted. He held nothing back from anybody.

"Come to me, *all* you who are weary and burdened," He said, "and I will give you rest. Take my yoke upon you and learn from me, for I am gentle and humble in heart, and you will find rest for your souls. For my yoke is easy and my burden is light."

Rest! That is what they all wanted. Rest from pain, rest from sorrow, rest from worry.

"Come!" He pleaded, "all of you, come!"

They came; and as they listened to Him their poor, sad hearts were comforted.

One day word reached Jesus that Peter's mother-in-law was

ill. Busy as He was, He went straight to her house. The poor woman was very sick with "a high fever." Jesus took one look at her, then tenderly touched her hand. Immediately "the fever left her," and her strength returned. A moment later she was up and about, waiting on her visitors.

That same evening "when the sun was setting, the people brought to Jesus all who had various kinds of sickness, and laying his hands on each one, he healed them.

"Moreover, demons came out of many people, shouting, 'You are the Son of God.' "

What a time that was! Earth had never seen anything like it. The God of love was making Himself known, letting everybody see how kind and good and tenderhearted and forgiving He really was.

He had told Moses long before that "the Lord, the Lord" is "the compassionate and gracious God, slow to anger, abounding in love and faithfulness, maintaining love to thousands, and forgiving wickedness, rebellion and sin." * Now everybody could see with their own eyes. From now on there could be no doubt. God in Christ was all that love could be.

---

* Exodus 34:6, 7.

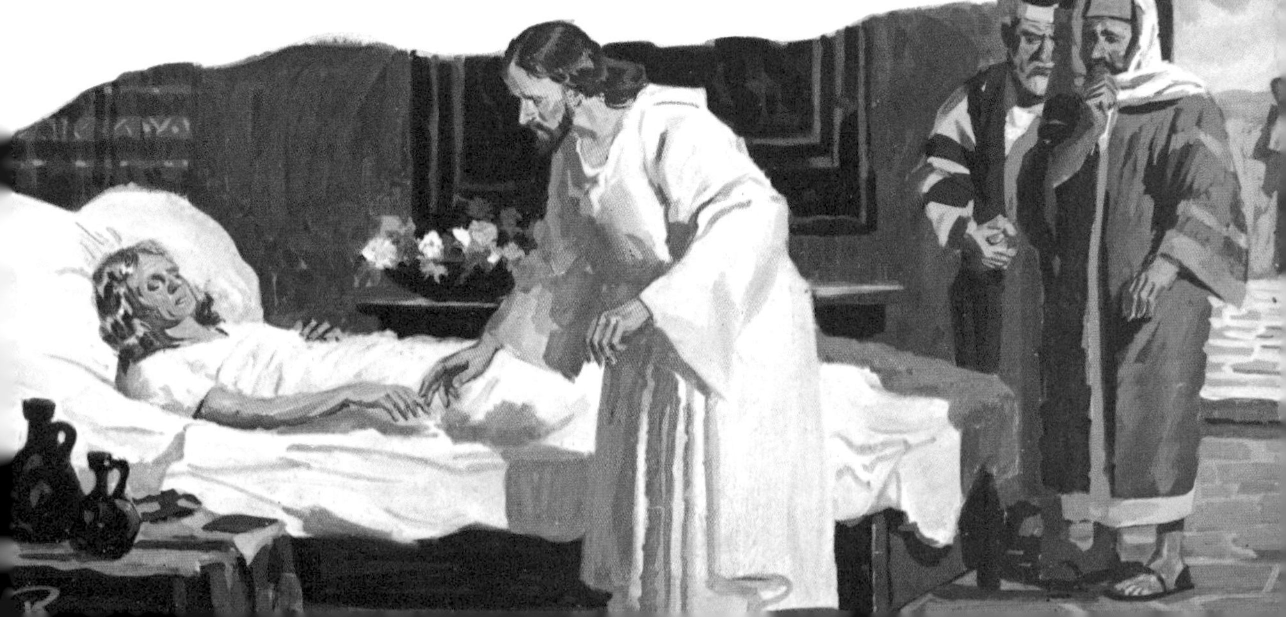

Hometown Boy Returns

(Luke 4:16-30)

AFTER some time Jesus came to Nazareth again. How glad He must have been to see His old hometown once more! No doubt He looked in the carpenter's shop where He had spent so many busy, happy years. Perhaps He thought it would be nice to open His toolbox and start making something again. But there was no time for that now.

Hardly had He arrived in town when people began to crowd around Him. They wanted to see how He had changed since He had left home. Because He had grown up with them, they found it hard to believe the stories they had heard about His preaching and healing. Others might think He was the Son of God, but here He was just the son of Joseph.

When it was rumored that Jesus might speak in the synagogue on Sabbath, everybody flocked to hear Him. As He rose to read from the Holy Scriptures, He looked out over the largest congregation that had ever packed the place. Most of the faces were familiar to Him. He had known these people all His life. Some were friendly, others critical, but all were curious to hear

← PAINTING BY PAUL REMMEY

When Jesus returned to His home town of Nazareth, the fame of His teaching and healing had gone before Him, and now everyone flocked to the synagogue to hear Him speak.

what the "hometown boy" would say.

Jesus had worshiped in this synagogue all His early life. More than 1,000 times He must have walked here from His home on the Sabbath day, first with Joseph and Mary, then with Mary alone, and sometimes by Himself. That is why the Bible says that when He came to Nazareth now, He went into the synagogue on the Sabbath day "as was his custom." It had been His custom for a long, long time, and this day He gladly followed it again.

Opening the Scriptures to the book of Isaiah, Jesus began to read from chapter 61. There, according to Luke 4:18, 19, it says: "The Spirit of the Lord is on me, because he has anointed me to preach good news to the poor. He has sent me to proclaim freedom for the prisoners and recovery of sight for the blind, to release the oppressed, to proclaim the year of the Lord's favor."

Jesus read the old familiar words so tenderly, yet forcefully, that everybody was moved by them. When He closed the scroll, "the eyes of everyone in the synagogue were fastened on him." Then He shocked them by saying, "Today this scripture is fulfilled in your hearing."

As the people listened in amazement He applied this famous prophecy to Himself. "I, who have lived among you so long," He said in effect, "have been anointed by God to do this work and preach this message. Once I mended your furniture, but now I shall mend broken hearts, give sight to the blind, and set the oppressed at liberty."

At first the beauty of His words and the gentleness of His voice captured the hearts of the people so much that they "were

amazed at the gracious words that came from his lips." Then a change came.

Many of the people hoped He would perform a miracle, as He had in Capernaum and other places. When they heard Him say that God had sent Him to deliver captives and give sight to the blind they felt sure that He would heal somebody then and there. But He didn't.

So they began to criticize Him. "Isn't this Joseph's son?" they whispered. "He's nobody after all! He can't work miracles."

Jesus knew what was going on in their minds and said, "I know you are saying, 'Physician, heal yourself.' Do what you did in Capernaum here, too. But 'no prophet is accepted in his hometown.' "

Then He reminded them that in the days of Elijah it was a widow of *Sidon*, not of Israel, who was fed in the years of famine; and that in the days of Elisha it was Naaman, a *Syrian*, who was healed of leprosy, though there were many lepers in Israel.

What He wanted them to see was that it is not the place where a person lives that matters to God, but the state of his heart. God's miracles are for those of *any* city or *any* nation who believe in Him and do what He says. The people of Nazareth didn't believe Jesus was sent from God, and so He couldn't help them.

The people got the point at once. It made them angry. "So He thinks we're not as good as the people of Capernaum!" they whispered. "Well, we'll show Him."

Suddenly the peace and calm of the holy Sabbath was

shattered. Men jumped to their feet, shouting at the Preacher. Some left their seats and rushed toward Him. Soon the whole synagogue was in turmoil.

Jesus managed to make His way out safely, but once on the street He found Himself facing a huge, angry crowd.

"Kill Him!" cried somebody. "Shove Him over the cliff!"

The mob began pushing Jesus to the high ridge near which Nazareth was built. Things looked bad for a while. It seemed as if Jesus' ministry was going to end almost before it had begun.

But suddenly the crowd stopped in confusion. People started shouting at each other, "Where is He? Where's He gone?"

Jesus had disappeared. The Bible says that "he walked right through the crowd and went on his way."

So He left Nazareth. But what a pity that His own city, the place of His childhood and youth, had treated Him like this! Much as He had wanted to help these people, He couldn't. They wouldn't let Him. A few were blessed by His coming. Jesus was able to "lay his hands on a few sick people and heal them." But "he did not do many miracles there because of their lack of faith."

How much they missed by their meanness and disbelief!

The Master Fisherman

(Luke 5:1-11)

SOME years ago I stood on the shore of Lake Galilee and watched the fishing boats come in. It was early in the morning. The sun was rising over the eastern hills, throwing a golden glow over the dark, still water.

Then through the mist came the little boats. First one, then another. They were steering for the jetty at Tiberias, where at last they all tied up.

I walked on the jetty and looked in the boats. Some had a few fish in them; some had none. The fishermen hadn't had a very successful night, and I couldn't help thinking of that morning long ago when Jesus stood on this very spot. That was when Peter and his friends had also had a bad night's fishing. Not a bite! Not a single fish in their nets!

Coming ashore, they had just begun to wash their nets and get ready for the next night's fishing when they noticed Jesus coming toward them, followed by a crowd of people. As Jesus stopped near the water's edge, the crowd pressed closer and closer until He was in danger of being pushed into the lake.

Seeing a boat pulled up on the shore He stepped into it and asked Peter, who was standing nearby, to shove it out a little way.

Peter gladly did, and Jesus "sat down and taught the people from the boat." What a beautiful scene that must have been, as the little boats rolled gently back and forth on the quiet waves, their sails flapping idly in the breeze. The bright morning sunshine lighted the lovely countryside and mixed a million diamonds in the tiny wavelets that lapped the shore.

On the beach sat scores of men and women, old and young, rich and poor, looking eagerly into the face of Jesus, loving every precious word that fell from His lips. In front of them may have been a couple of little girls paddling in the water and a boy

PAUL REMMEY, ARTIST

trying to float a boat he had cut from a piece of wood. But even they were listening, looking up now and then in the hope that Jesus would smile at them.

How long Jesus spoke we do not know. At last, however, He told the people it was time for them to go. Then, turning to Peter, He said, "Put out into deep water, and let down the nets for a catch."

Peter looked at Him in surprise. Didn't He know that nobody went fishing in the daytime? Jesus might be a wonderful teacher, but He must surely be a very poor fisherman.

"Master," he said, "we've worked hard all night and haven't caught anything. But because you say so, I will let down the nets."

He had no hope of catching any fish at this time of the morning, but he was willing to do anything to please this good, kind Man. So he and his friends hauled up the anchor and began to row. They didn't go far. It didn't seem worthwhile. After all, they were only going fishing to humor the Master.

The men stopped rowing and threw the net overboard. I am sure there must have been a smile on Jesus' face as they did. He knew what was going to happen. Pretty soon they would find out that He wasn't such a bad fisherman after all.

Meanwhile the men sat around wondering how long they should wait before pulling in the net. They didn't want to do it too soon, of course; that wouldn't seem very polite. But finally

Peter said, "Better bring it in now," and they all started hauling on the ropes.

Suddenly their eyes opened wide in astonishment. The net was as heavy as lead. They had to heave and pull with all their might just to move it a few inches. It was full of fish!

"Look out!" cried Peter. "The net's breaking!"

And so it was. Their strong, well-made net, of which they had been so proud, was splitting right before their eyes.

"Help!" they cried excitedly to fishermen in another boat nearby. "Come! Help us get these fish on board!"

The men in the other boat got out their oars and rowed their hardest toward them. Soon the men in both boats were wrestling with that bursting net, trying to heave it out of the water. Some of the fish were tipped into one boat, some into the other. This went on until both boats were "so full that they began to sink."

With water lapping over the sides of the boats, the men rowed for the shore. And when they got there, what do you suppose they did? They forgot all about the fish and the nets and the boats, and fell on their knees before Jesus.

"Go away from me, Lord; I am a sinful man!" Peter said humbly.

"Don't be afraid," Jesus said to him. "From now on you will catch men."

Their hearts were won. They "left everything and followed him."

The Man With Five Friends

(Luke 5:17-26)

ONE DAY Jesus was invited into a very nice home in Capernaum to meet some famous people. Pharisees and "teachers of the law" had gathered here "from every village of Galilee and from Judea and Jerusalem."

These church leaders had heard a great deal about Jesus, and they wanted to meet Him. The whole countryside was talking about this new Teacher and Healer, and they felt that they must find out about Him for themselves.

Most of them no doubt were old men, with long, gray beards. Jesus, only 30 years old, must have seemed quite young beside them. Can't you see them peering at Him with keen, critical eyes, wondering how this humble-looking Carpenter of Nazareth could do the things people said He had done?

At last Jesus began to speak, but it was difficult to make Himself heard. There were so many people outside clamoring to get in. It seemed as if the whole town knew He was there and wanted to be near Him and listen to His words.

Suddenly something extraordinary happened. The roof began to disappear! Looking up, the Pharisees and teachers of the law saw several pairs of hands hurriedly taking the tiles off the roof! Then, to their amazement, down came a bed, lowered on ropes held by four men. Down, down, it came until it was right in the middle of everybody.

On the bed was a very sick man, so paralyzed he could scarcely move.

Some of the important men were very annoyed. Some, no doubt, said, "Take him away! Get him out of here at once."

But the sick man was lying helpless on his bed, and Jesus' tender heart was full of pity for him. Knowing the true cause of the poor man's sickness, Jesus said to him, "Friend, your sins are forgiven."

"Blasphemy!" whispered one of the old men. "Who can forgive sins, but God alone?"

Jesus knew what they were all thinking and asked them, "Which is easier: to say, 'Your sins are forgiven,' or to say, 'Get up and walk'?"

None of them could answer Him. So Jesus told them He would let them see that the Son of man had power on earth to forgive sins. Turning to the sick man, He told him to get up, take up his bed, and go home.

Instantly the man leaped to his feet, perfectly well, and ran away "praising God."

I hope he stopped long enough to thank his friends. For he had five of them. The four who had let him down through the roof and Jesus, who had restored him to health and strength.

As for the old men, "everyone was amazed and gave praise to God. They were filled with awe and said, 'We have seen remarkable things today.' "

The Centurion's Servant

(Matthew 8:5-13; Luke 7:1-10)

ONE DAY while Jesus was in Capernaum, an officer in the Roman army asked for His help. He was a centurion, which means that he was commander of a company of 100 soldiers. Most likely he was the most important Roman officer in the city.

As an officer, it was his duty to keep the peace. He had been watching Jesus ever since He first came to Capernaum and began His work. He had stood in the crowd and listened as Jesus taught the people. It had been his duty to make sure that this Galilean wasn't saying anything that might lead the people to rebel against Rome.

As he had listened he had come to respect Jesus very highly. Here, he was sure, was a very good Man and a very great Man. The kingdom of love He talked about was no threat to Rome. Rome could do with some of this love.

When his servant became ill and the doctors could do nothing more for him, the centurion thought of Jesus and remembered the stories of His power to heal the sick.

But, he wondered, would Jesus be willing to help an officer in the hated Roman army? Did His love reach beyond the Jews? Well, it was worth trying.

First, he sent to the Jewish leaders and asked them to speak to Jesus for him. They did, adding that this man was worthy of help "because he loves our nation and has built our synagogue."

But the centurion didn't think he was worthy. As Jesus approached his house, he sent a messenger to say, very humbly, "Lord, don't trouble yourself, for I do not deserve to have you come under my roof. That is why I did not even consider myself worthy to come to you. But say the word, and my servant will be healed. For I myself am a man under authority, with soldiers under me. I tell this one, 'Go,' and he goes; and that one, 'Come,' and he comes. I say to my servant, 'Do this,' and he does it."

Hearing this, Jesus was amazed, and turning to those about Him said, "I have not found such great faith even in Israel."

This centurion, a Roman soldier, was the first to see that Jesus was not only a Healer and a Teacher but a Ruler and a King. He had seen more in Jesus than the Jews, to whom He had come as Messiah. That is why Jesus went on to say, "Many will come from the east and the west, and will take their places at the feast with Abraham, Isaac and Jacob in the kingdom of heaven. But the subjects of the kingdom will be thrown outside."

By this He meant that people of many nations and countries will accept Him as their Lord, while others nearby, who should know better, will reject Him.

Pleased by the centurion's amazing faith and wishing to teach His hearers a lesson, Jesus turned to him and said, "Go! It will be done just as you believed it would."

The centurion had said that he believed Jesus could heal his servant at a distance, without even coming to the house. He was sure Jesus just had to say the word, and the sick man would be healed. And that's what happened. As soon as Jesus commended the centurion for his faith, at that very moment his servant was healed.

I can imagine the servant jumping out of his bed, his pain all gone, his face wreathed in smiles. "Thank you, thank you!" I can hear him saying to his master.

"Don't thank me," I am sure the noble centurion replied. "Thank the wonderful Carpenter of Nazareth."

The Interrupted Funeral

(Luke 7:11-17)

SOON after He had healed the centurion's servant, to the surprise of His friends, Jesus left Capernaum for the little city of Nain, some 20 miles (32 kilometers) away. This meant a long uphill climb, and His disciples, who walked beside and behind Him, must have wondered why He had suddenly decided to go on this tiring trip. They did not know that a widow's son had just died in Nain, but Jesus did.

As they trudged along the rugged mountain trail the group of followers grew larger and larger until, as the Bible says, "a large crowd went along with him." There was magic in the name of Jesus. Workers in the fields dropped their tools and hurried to join the passing procession. Women ran out of their houses at the sound of His voice. The sick followed too, leaning on friends, hoping to be healed. Boys and girls came in droves to see what was going on. It was a great day for everybody.

THE INTERRUPTED FUNERAL

As the big crowd came near to Nain, another procession came out of the city gate. It was a funeral. One group was following the Prince of life; the other a dead body on its way to the cemetery. One was made up of happy, expectant people; the other of weeping, despairing ones. It was like a river of life flowing into a river of death. Something was bound to happen.

From the size of the funeral procession, it seemed as though almost all the people in the city must have decided to show their respect for the dead youth and their sympathy for his mother, who was a widow. Everyone was sad that she had lost her only son.

Could it be that Jesus was acquainted with this poor woman and her son? Why not? And did He time His arrival at Nain to bring her help just when hope seemed gone? He knows so much about all of us, and He loves and cares for us so deeply!

As the two processions met, Jesus came face-to-face with the poor widow. She was walking close behind the ones who carried her dead boy, and she was weeping bitterly.

As Jesus stopped to speak to her the crowd behind Him surged forward. A moment later He, the woman, and the dead boy, were in the center of a seething mass of people, all trying to see what was going on.

"Don't cry," Jesus said to the widow, in deep compassion. And there was something in His voice that seemed to say, "You don't need to cry anymore; I have a surprise for you."

Now His voice rang like a command. "Young man, I say to you, get up."

Suddenly the dead youth moved. His eyes opened. Then he sat up and began to talk. Terrified, the pallbearers fled into the crowd. The next moment mother and son were in each other's arms, weeping tears of joy at this wonderful event.

Those who saw the astounding miracle were struck with awe. The look of amazement on their faces must have been something to see. For a while everybody—men and women, boys and girls—was speechless. Then the silence was broken by a murmur that grew louder and louder as one person passed

the news to another, clear to the back of the crowd.

"He raised the dead!" people whispered. "He even raised the dead!"

"He told the boy to come to life, and he did!"

"He gave the widow back her son! How kind of Him!"

"He stopped a funeral! Whoever heard of such a thing!"

" 'A great prophet has appeared among us,' they said. 'God has come to help his people.' "

Meanwhile the widow and her son were struggling to make their way back to the city through the crowds of people who were trying to catch a glimpse of them.

How happy they were! Jesus had turned their night into day, their sorrow into joy.

Lord of the Winds and Waves

(Matthew 8:23-27)

ONE EVENING, after a busy day of teaching and healing, Jesus said to His disciples, "Let's get in a boat and go to the other side of the lake." He was tired, and longed to get away to some quiet spot where He could rest awhile.

But it was hard to persuade the people to go home. They just stayed and stayed and stayed, enjoying every minute in His presence. Like children at bedtime, they kept on asking for more and more stories. At last, however, the disciples made them understand that Jesus simply couldn't talk to them anymore that day. He just had to have a rest.

As the crowds began to drift away, the disciples helped Jesus "just as he was" into one of the boats and pushed off from the land. Other little boats set off at the same time, no doubt filled with people who had made up their minds to follow Him wherever He might go.

Tired out, Jesus went to the back of the boat and lay down on a pillow. A moment later He was fast asleep.

LORD OF THE WINDS AND WAVES

It was a beautiful evening. The sun went down behind the western hills in a blaze of glory. Darkness fell, and the stars came out. A gentle breeze filled the sails, carrying all the boats toward the land of Gadara.

Then suddenly the weather changed, as it does on the Sea of Galilee even today. In less time than it takes to tell, a storm swept down the mountains, turning the peaceful lake into a wild and dangerous sea. Dark clouds rushed across the sky, blotting out the stars. Thunder roared. Lightning flashed. The breeze became a fierce gale, whipping up great waves that swept over the boats, filling them with water.

The storm was so bad that even Peter, James, John, and the other disciples who had grown up on the lake were frightened. It was the worst night they had ever known. Despair

seized them. They felt sure this was the end.

Then they remembered Jesus.

Oddly enough, He was still asleep. Even the loudest thunderclaps had not awakened Him, and the fearful rolling and tossing had not disturbed Him.

The water rose higher and higher in the boat, despite their best efforts to bail it out. The disciples could not stand it any longer. They had to wake Jesus up. Shouting above the roaring wind, one of them cried, "Teacher, don't you care if we drown?"

Jesus stood up, His feet in the water that was sloshing from side to side in the boat.

"Lord, save us! We're going to drown!" cried the disciples—a cry Jesus never fails to answer.

Looking around at the dark, angry sky and the frightening white-capped waves, He said, in a voice of command, "Quiet! Be still!"

Suddenly, as quickly as it had come up, the storm died away "and it was completely calm."

In words of gentle rebuke Jesus said to His disciples, "Why are you so afraid? Do you still have no faith?"

There was nothing they could say to this. They just went on bailing out the water, whispering in awe to one another, "What kind of man is this? Even the winds and the waves obey him!"

No wonder! Never had they heard anyone order the elements about like this. Nothing like this had ever happened since Creation, when God said, "Let there be light," "Let there

◆ PAINTING BY WILLIAM HUTCHINSON

As the great storm swept over the Sea of Galilee, and threatened to capsize the boat, the disciples cried out in fear. Then Jesus calmed the tempest with the words "Peace, be still."

be an expanse," "Let the water teem with living creatures," "Let the land produce living creatures according to their kinds." * Now the Creator had spoken again, and Creation had recognized His voice.

What happened to all the people in the other little boats? The Bible does not say. But they must have had a very bad time. If the disciples had been afraid, I am sure they were too. They must have also cried for help, and when the great calm came, they were very relieved.

Perhaps Jesus was thinking of them too when He told the wind and waves to be still. I believe He was, because He never forgets the people in the other little boats.

In all the storms of life Jesus is never far away. The little prayer "Lord, save me!" will bring Him swiftly to our rescue.

* Genesis 1:3-24.

Madmen Made Sane

(Matthew 8:28-34; Mark 5:20; Luke 8:26-38)

AS MORNING dawned, calm and beautiful, the boat in which Jesus and His disciples had crossed the lake glided into a sheltered cove on the eastern shore. Everything seemed so peaceful after the wild, terrible night, that everyone on board looked forward to a quiet and restful day.

But that's not what happened. Hardly had they started up the trail into the foothills when two demon-possessed men, who had been hiding among the tombs in a cemetery, rushed out at them.

They were a frightening sight. Madness was in their eyes and voices. Blood flowed over their naked bodies where they had cut themselves with stones. Broken chains, fastened to their wrists and ankles, clanked as they ran.

Most people would have fled in terror from such hideous, dangerous men. But not Jesus. He was not afraid of anybody or anything. He could sleep through a storm at sea or stand calmly while a couple of demon-possessed men ran toward Him.

The demons in the men recognized Jesus right away. "What do you want with us, O Son of God?" they cried. "Have you come here to torture us before the appointed time?"

They knew that Christ was their Master and that they were powerless in His presence. They knew, too, that He would cast them out of the men whose minds they now controlled. So they asked if they could enter a herd of pigs that was feeding nearby.

Jesus gave permission, and suddenly the herd of pigs became as mad as the two men had been. Charging crazily this way and that, they plunged at last over a cliff into the lake and were drowned.

Those tending the pigs, afraid they would be blamed for

the loss of the animals, hurried with the news to the town nearby. Very upset, the people came running to find out what had happened. They saw an amazing sight. Their pigs had disappeared, but the two madmen, who for years had been the terror of the neighborhood, were sitting at the feet of Jesus, clothed and in their right minds.

Perhaps the disciples had shared their own clothes with them and helped them clean up in the waters of the lake. In any case, here they were, perfectly sane and normal.

The city people were frightened and begged Jesus to go away. They were afraid they might lose more of their pigs if He stayed around much longer. It did not occur to them—at least, not then—that if He stayed with them, He might bring help to other people in need.

They made so much fuss that Jesus agreed to leave at once. As He walked down to the boat, the two men He had healed begged to be allowed to go along with Him.

But Jesus would not let them. "No," He said. "Go home to your family and tell them how much the Lord has done for you, and how he has had mercy on you."

So they stood on the shore and waved goodbye as the boat sailed away. Then they did as Jesus had told them. They went

back home and told everybody "how much Jesus had done" for them.

They were the first missionaries Jesus ever sent out, and certainly among the best. They told their story so well that soon everybody for miles around was talking about Jesus and longing to see Him. Those who had asked Him to go away were ashamed of what they had done. And when Jesus returned to Gadara some time later, they were all expecting Him and a crowd welcomed Him.

It just shows how much two people can do when they start talking about the great things Jesus has done for them. These two men who had once been demon-possessed made all the people of Gadara long to meet Jesus.

Has Jesus done something great for you? Has He shown His love for you in one way or another? Has He given you a "right mind" when you were being angry or foolish? Has He helped you to get rid of some bad habit? Then why not tell everybody about it?

Who knows what the result may be? Your brave witness may lead thousands to Him.